MW01282112

TO:

_____

FROM:

_____

DATE:

_____

Moments
of Grace
— FOR GRANDMAS —

*Stories & Scriptures to Warm
Your Heart & Refresh Your Soul*

Carol Kent, General Editor
and Gracie Malone

Christian Art
PUBLISHERS

Visit Christian Art Gifts, Inc., at www.christianartgifts.com.

Moments of Grace for Grandmas: Stories & Scriptures to Warm Your Heart & Refresh Your Soul

Previously published by Zondervan as *Kisses of Sunshine for Grandmas* © 2005.
Content revised and updated in 2025 by Carol Kent and Gracie Malone.

Published by Christian Art Gifts, Inc., IL, USA.

First edition 2025.

Designed by Christian Art Gifts, Inc.

Cover and interior images used under license from Shutterstock.com

Most Christian Art titles may be purchased at bulk discounts by churches, nonprofits, and corporations. For more information, please email SpecialMarkets@cagifts.com.

ISBN 978-1-63952-893-6

Printed in China.

30 29 28 27 26 25
10 9 8 7 6 5 4 3 2 1

To
Luke, Connor, Mary, Abby, Montana,
Myles, Zoe Sofia, and Mia Grace.

– Gracie Malone –

To
Chelsea and Hannah

– Carol Kent –

Other Books in the Moments of Grace Series

Contents

Introduction

This series of five books—one each for grandmas, moms, sisters, teachers, and women—has lighthearted, uplifting, and often humorous stories meant to bring a sunburst of joy to your life as you remember that God loves you. Gracie Malone has joined me in putting these stories together, and our purpose is simply to let God's grace so fill you that you become warmth, light, and love to a cold, dark world.

The writer, Teresa Bloomingdale, reportedly said, "If your baby is beautiful and perfect, never cries or fusses, sleeps on schedule and burps on demand, an angel all the time—you're the grandma." On a personal note, there is nothing that brings me more pleasure than spending time with my granddaughters. I have their pictures in my wallet and their drawings on my refrigerator. I pray for them every day and envision what they might "be" when they grow up.

Having taught speech and drama, I look forward to their dramatic productions where I become "an audience of one," applauding their puppet shows and cheering after their living room musical productions. I think Chelsea and Hannah are as close to "professional actresses" as children can be, and I am convinced their IQs are higher than most elementary school kids.

Yes, I'm prejudiced, because I am a grandma—and that

gives me every right to brag, exaggerate, and overstate their accomplishments. I know they are the best, the smartest, the most well behaved, the prettiest, and the most charming of all children. I should know—they're *mine*!

The coauthor of this book is Gracie Malone. If her name sounds familiar, it's because she's an expert in the art of grandparenting and her book *Off My Rocker* is a favorite of grandparents everywhere. Gracie has more stories than almost anyone I know, and she tells them in a manner that makes me grab my stomach because I'm laughing so hard I can hardly sit still while I'm reading. Gracie is not only funny, she's filled with wisdom, love, and compassion. You'll get to know Grandma Gracie very personally as you read this book—and you'll be a better grandma, too, because her techniques work. Both of us deeply appreciate Rob Teigen and the creative team at Christian Art Gifts for giving us the privilege of working on such a delightful project.

I'm also grateful to the remarkable women who shared their own grandparenting stories in this book. You made me laugh and cry—and you reminded me that I don't have to be perfect to be a good grandma. William James once said, "The great use of life is to spend it on something that will outlast it." I'm spending my life investing time in my grandchildren. I hope this book inspires you to do the same.

Carol Kent
General Editor

My Children's Children
– Gracie Malone –

Before you were born, I loved you.
Before you were here one hour,
I would give my life for you.

Maureen Hawkins, from "Miracle of Life"

One morning our oldest son, Matt, called with the news I'd been waiting for. "If you hurry," he blurted out, "you can make it for the birth of your grandson." I jumped in the car and headed for the hospital.

The drive from our hometown of Greenville to theirs in Carrollton would take almost an hour. On the way, my heart beat at a faster than usual pace as I thought about the new baby as well as the new role my children would be assuming. It was fun to imagine Matt as a daddy and Rebecca as a mom. I knew they would be good parents. And I couldn't wait to meet the newest member of our clan.

I whipped into a parking place, pushed through the front door of Trinity Medical Center, and headed down the hall toward the maternity wing. Rounding the corner into the waiting room, I spotted Matt dressed in hospital scrubs, a surgical mask hanging loosely around his neck. Apparently, the childbirth classes had prepared him to be a fully participating member of the delivery team.

With a broad sweep of his hand, he motioned me onward. "Follow me!" Pushing through the swinging doors, he escorted me down the hall and into the birthing room.

Rebecca was nestled in a contraption that looked more like Joe's recliner than a hospital bed. She looked tired, but, to my surprise, was fully awake and smiling as she extended a tiny bundle in my direction. "Want to hold him?" she asked.

Yes! Of course, I did.

I gently took Baby Luke from his mother's arms and pulled him close to my bosom. He was only minutes old. The tiny little boy felt warm as he wiggled and stretched. I'd forgotten how small a newborn baby is, barely big enough to fit in the crook of a woman's arm. As I gazed into his slate-blue eyes, straining to focus in the soft light, I was suddenly overcome with emotion—the same feelings I'd experienced when I held my own newborn sons—love, joy, hope, and a swelling sense of pride. I swallowed hard, choking back the lump rising in my throat.

My eyes examined the features of my newborn grandson—a perfect heart-shaped mouth, tiny, upturned nose, a slight crimp on both ears. I folded back the corner of the blue flannel blanket that swaddled him and touched his hand. When four tiny, wrinkled fingers curled around one of my own, I knew I was hooked for life. I blinked back a tear as I marveled at the wonder of God's creation and the blessing of this gift.

I remembered a verse from Psalms describing a developing baby as "intricately and curiously wrought [as if embroidered with various colors]" (Psalm 139:15, AMPC). The thought that God, the awesome creator of the universe, had been "intricately" involved in the design of my precious grandson brought tears of joy to my eyes.

I lifted the tiny bundle close to my lips and whispered against the soft folds of skin, "Luke, I'm your grandmother. I love you. I always will, no matter what."

With the birth of this little boy, our family had come full circle, making our own revolution in the great circle of life. A new generation was born that day—one that would bear our name.

Since the birth of Luke, I've been in the waiting room during the arrival of several additional grandchildren. Luke was barely three when his parents presented him with a little brother, Connor. They in turn welcomed two little sisters, Mary and Abby. Our son Mike and daughter-in-law Jeanna blessed us with two little boys—Montana and Myles. A few years later, son Jason and daughter-in-law Junipa added two granddaughters, Zoe and Mia. And this year the Malone clan added our first great-grandson, David Owen.

Each child came into the world with unique features, characteristics, and temperaments. And with the birth of each child, the promise of a brighter future and hope for tomorrow was reborn in my heart. Whenever I hold a new-born grandchild in my arms, why, I feel newborn myself.

> *You made all the delicate inner parts of my*
> *body and knit me together in my mother's womb.*
> *Thank you for making me so wonderfully complex!*
> *Your workmanship is marvelous—how well I know it.*

PSALM 139:13–14 NLT

Mrs. McGillicutty's Band-Aids

— Luan Zemmer Jackson, MS, RN, CS —

Everybody should try to have a grandmother,
especially if they don't have a television, iPhone, or iPad,
because they are the only grown-ups who have time.

Excerpt from an essay by a third-grade student from Langley, BC

When I was two-and-a-half years old, my father was the pastor of a small country church. On weekdays he was a medical student in the city, and on weekends he returned home to tend to his church duties. We lived in a small country house, and life was hard.

My grandma (the bright spot in my life) lived across the road. Every day I would dress up in my best outfit and knock on her door. Grandma greeted me as if I were the most important company she ever entertained. She had a magnificent imagination and created imaginary scenarios that took me far beyond my current circumstances.

Our favorite game transformed us into neighbors. Grandma was Mrs. McGillicutty, and I was Mrs. Zemmer. In European style we had tea and talked about our children. (Grandma had six children, and I had my dolls.) I always felt important and grown-up when I visited Grandma. She asked for my advice on dealing with her problems and listened intently to my answers. I knew Grandma loved me and valued my advice.

Rainy days made me a prisoner at home and kept Grandma's world out of reach. On one occasion, after several days of rain, I persuaded my mother to let me go to Grandma's. As I crossed the road, I fell into a massive mud puddle. Sitting in that cold, murky water, covered with slimy muck, I started to cry. Embarrassment and shame overwhelmed me. How could I have been so careless? My good dress was filthy. My knee was scraped and hurting. What would Grandma say?

From her yard on the other side of the road, Grandma saw my plight, came across the road, and rescued me. With a smile she said, "Don't cry, Luan, we'll get you all cleaned up. Your dress will be just fine, and we'll put a Band-Aid on you."

Grandma talked to me as she was cleaning my wounds. "Luan, I want you to remember how embarrassed you feel—and how your knee hurts. Other people hurt sometimes too. It feels good to have someone take care of you, doesn't it? Remember that others have hurts and need to be cared for."

After that incident I became a "ministering angel." I started a doll hospital. My friends played house with their dolls, but I had a new mission—to help people who needed my services. I waited for someone to get hurt—a neighbor, family member, or stranger—and rushed in to cleanse the wound and apply a Band-Aid.

In those days of economic hardship, money was precious, but Grandma kept me well supplied with Band-Aids. Well-meaning adults told Grandma she was wasting valuable resources to buy Band-Aids for a child to play with, but she continued to supply me with resources for my little nurse's bag. Because of Grandma, whenever someone had a wound, I would confidently care for them. Grandma's words still ring in my ears, "You are so caring, Luan. It's comforting to have you here to take care of us!"

Mrs. McGillicutty and Mrs. Zemmer continued to have tea together for many years. Grandma helped me envision an exciting and fulfilling future. "When you grow up," she said, "you will be a great nurse, because nurses are caring just like you and they take care of hurting people just like you do." In between sips of tea, she complimented me on my communication skills and encouraged my sense of humor. "In a world full of pain, we need to laugh and help others to laugh," she would say with a chuckle.

Somewhere between having tea and distributing Band-Aids, I determined that with God's help (and Grandma's encouragement), I would get an education. Grandma had been honest about her poor choices. "When I was young," she told me, "I listened to my friends talking about marriage. I wanted to be a nurse, but I hid my dream and did what everyone else was doing. Marriage is wonderful, but you need an education first. In order to be a good nurse, you will need to attend college." She added, "Never give up!"

Grandma saw beyond the little girl in the mud puddle and believed in my potential. She gave wings to my dreams by supplying me with Band-Aids. And she passed on a legacy of love that is being transferred to the next generation through my children today.

By the way, Mrs. Zemmer *did* become a nurse, and when she grew up, she operated a full-service mental health clinic. And she misses having tea with Mrs. McGillicutty.

*The people brought children to Jesus, hoping he
might touch them. The disciples shooed them off.
But Jesus was irate and let them know it: "Don't push
these children away. Don't ever get between them and me.
These children are at the very center of life in the kingdom.
Mark this: Unless you accept God's kingdom in the simplicity
of a child, you'll never get in." Then, gathering the children
up in his arms, he laid his hands of blessing on them.*

MARK 10:13–16 MSG

Terms of Endearment

— Gracie Malone —

I don't care what you call me; just call me.

Anonymous

When our grandson Luke started babbling, all ears perked up. "Dah-d-d-d-dah, M-m-m-m-m, Mah!" Eventually the jabbered syllables became words—the ones he would use to identify his parents. Little Luke didn't say the usual toddler words, "Dada" or "Mama." Oh, no! One day while munching on a handful of Cheerios, he nonchalantly looked up at my daughter-in-law and addressed her in a very grown-up manner as "Mom." A few days later he pronounced my son his "Dad." We were elated. After two years of parental coaxing, Luke could talk. Now, I wondered, what would he call me?

My mother is "Me Ma"—a name lovingly bestowed on her by grandson number one. My friend Carol is "Mia." I know one "Mimi," two "Grams" and a "G-mother." One of my friends is addressed with the very British sounding "Grandma-ma." My sister Lois is identified by the conventional title "Grandmother." Even the youngest of her grandkids is able to mouth the distinguished-sounding term. Lois is delighted. In her opinion, *grandmother* is "the most beautiful word a grandchild can say."

One afternoon Lois explained to me how the grandmother titling process works. "You see," she began, "it's Luke's choice. No matter what you call yourself, he will make his own selection, and, most likely, your future grandchildren will follow suit. Don't worry about it, Gracie. Whatever he calls you, I'm sure it will be just perfect." With that bit of information safely tucked away in my memory bank, I waited and I wondered.

Then one day, just as Lois predicted, when I was stacking blocks with Luke, it happened. He placed his block atop the leaning tower we'd built on my living room floor, grinned, and started to speak, "Gr-r-r-r ..." My heart skipped a beat as I waited for the word "gr-r-r-andma" or "gr-r-r-andmother" to come from his peanut-butter-covered mouth. But his enunciation was perfectly clear as he said, "Gr-r-r-acie."

I have to admit I was a bit disappointed. I had hoped to have my grandchildren call me something more tender and, well ... unique and special. Maybe even something classy or cute. Nevertheless, I was delighted my grandson had spoken my name. And I thought perhaps my title would change as Luke's verbal skills developed; maybe it would even evolve into something a little more traditional.

It didn't happen.

Even when his parents coaxed and made suggestions,

my moniker stuck like a piece of gum on the bottom of my shoe. "Gr-r-racie," Luke would bellow, and in spite of feeling a bit chagrined at the grown-up manner the little tyke spoke my name, I'd come-a-runnin'.

Gracie is what Luke called me until his parents finally convinced him to add the title "Grandma." It just seemed the respectable thing to do. So today I am Luke's "Grandma Gracie." (I'm also "Grandma Gracie" to a whole passel of subsequent grandchildren.)

And I've decided my sister was right after all. "Grandma Gracie" was the perfect choice. In spite of the 50-year age gap between us, my grandson and I have a "Luke and Gracie" kind of relationship. A friendship—one I will cherish for the rest of my days.

A good name is to be more desired than great wealth;
Favor is better than silver and gold.

PROVERBS 22:1 NASB

A Tale of Two Angels

— Carol Kent —

Nobody can do for little children what grandparents do.
Grandparents sort of sprinkle stardust
over the lives of little children.

Alex Haley

The day had been exhilarating. During a break from speaking at an arena event in Denver, I called home for messages. Our son, a recent graduate of the U.S. Naval Academy, was in nuclear engineering school in Orlando, Florida. His voicemail communication was short: "Mom and Dad, some things are comin' down. We have to talk." Click.

When we got through to Jason several hours later, he picked up where he left off: "My naval orders have changed. I have to be at Surface Warfare Officers School in Newport, Rhode Island on September 8. April and I are in love, and we want to get married next Friday."

My heart leaped as I realized what I had just heard.

My son was asking to marry a woman I had never met *next Friday*! He was also telling me he planned to marry a previously married woman with *two children* next Friday!

I had trouble breathing, let alone talking, so my husband carried on the conversation as I dialogued with God.

Hello, God? Do you remember me? I've been praying for my son's future wife since he was in my womb. Lord, did you hear those prayers? This is not what I was anticipating!

Rational thinking returned slowly. We asked Jason and his new fiancée if they would wait three weeks and be married in our hometown with the accountability of family and friends around them. They agreed.

A week and a half later, Jason and April walked through our front door with their arms encircled around each other's waists. It didn't take me long to love April. She had been married at the age of sixteen to a man ten years her senior, and she had gone through more of "the tough stuff of life" than anyone deserves in a lifetime.

Behind the two of them, in walked six-year-old Chelsea and three-year-old Hannah. Within a half hour, sweet little Chelsea came running up to me. She took my hand in her two hands, made serious eye contact with me, and said, "You're my new favorite Grammy!" My heart melted.

Every morning, Hannah burst out of her bedroom with exuberance. She sat on a stool at my kitchen breakfast bar and ate her cereal, singing between every bite: "I love Jesus; he loves me! I love Jesus; he loves me!"

Within a matter of hours, these precious little girls had already won my heart.

As we prepared for the wedding, I enjoyed all the fun

of being an "instant Grammy." Chelsea and Hannah had full access to my closet, and they dressed up in long skirts, stiletto heels, sparkling necklaces, and colorful scarves. My two little angels danced and sang whenever they heard music in the background. They squealed with delight, and the house was filled with their infectious laughter and delightful questions.

"Grammy, pleeeeze, can I put on some of your lipstick?"

"Oh-h-h-h-h! Look at this dress! It has a flow-ee skirt. May I wear it?"

"I found Grammy's high heels! They are so-o-o beautiful. I'm going to look like a princess!"

"Oh, Grammy, can we fill your bathtub with bubbles and go swimming?"

"Do we *have* to go to bed? Please read us a story."

As the wedding day approached, I saw the deep love in the eyes of my son and his bride. And I already loved my big-brown-eyed granddaughters. I wasn't there for their births, but they were filling my heart with so much joy. Two little angels entered my life at an unexpected time and showered me with unconditional love and acceptance. I had a new name—*Grammy*! And I had a new passion—to be a godly influence in the lives of my granddaughters.

God *did* answer my prayer. But the answer came in a different package than I was expecting.

You're blessed when you stay on course,
walking steadily on the road revealed by GOD.

PSALM 119:1 MSG

Sweet Tarts

— Gracie Malone —

*Pretty much all the honest truth telling
there is in the world is done by children.*

Oliver Wendell Holmes Jr.

A few weeks before Christmas, my four-year-old-grandson Montana and I were flipping through some albums that contained pictures of his cousins—the children in our son Matt's family. Even though he hadn't seen his cousins in a long time, he identified all four—Luke, Connor, Mary, and Abby. After naming the children and commenting on their dressy clothes, he pointed to the main character. "And there's Uncle Matt!"

Next Montana pointed at the rather dignified gentleman in the center of the picture. He turned his face toward mine and with a cute little wrinkle in his forehead asked, "Grandma Gracie, who is that guy?"

"Oh, that man is the minister. We were at church," I explained to him.

Montana seemed confused. "The mister?"

"No, honey, the minister—you know, the *preacher.*"

"Oh!" The little guy seemed to understand as he turned the page.

Then he began naming the two people in the next shot. "There's Uncle Matt, and there's the *creature*."

Later I found myself chuckling about what Montana had said.

Shortly afterward, I had an interesting conversation with Montana's little brother, Myles. It seems Myles had developed a great relationship with the leadership at his church back home. I'd already heard that he never wanted to miss a single meeting at Fellowship of the Woodlands. I can't say I blame him when I think about the kid-friendly events that take place on that campus. Why, the excitement begins as soon as his parents pull into the enormous parking lot and then ride to the front door of the auditorium aboard a train made of brightly colored barrels. After they make their way inside and find a seat, serious business takes place.

Myles's fervor for toddler-style worship became evident one evening when our son Mike and daughter-in-law Jeanna were feeling a bit ambivalent about going to church. After lounging around the house most of Saturday afternoon, they couldn't get motivated to get dressed and go. Myles would hear nothing of it. He overheard their should-we-should-we-not conversation and decided for them.

"Well," he declared, "I'm going! You guys better get ready." He ran to his room and started changing clothes. What could Mike and Jeanna do but pull on some clean clothes and run to the car? When Jeanna told me this story later, my chest swelled with pride until I feared the buttons might pop off my blouse. My "strong-willed" little grandson had made a "strong" decision in the right direction and proved a truth that Jesus taught his disciples centuries ago. There are many times in our lives when "a little child shall lead them."

> "I thank you, Father, Master of heaven and earth,
> that you hid these things from the know-it-alls
> and showed them to these innocent newcomers.
> Yes, Father, it pleased you to do it this way."
>
> LUKE 10:21 MSG

The Magical White Sword

– Heidi McLaughlin –

Anything large enough for a wish to light upon,
is large enough to hang a prayer upon.

George MacDonald, from Unspoken Sermons

When my grandson Alex was three years old, he loved swords. Of course, his parents would not buy him one, but he improvised with anything he could find—a stick, creatively constructed LEGOs, or a wooden spoon. Alex is the middle child in a family of three energetic boys, and even though he was the quiet one, he had a way of tugging at my heart.

When the boys came to visit us that summer, I promised all three of them a trip to an adventure park. As soon as they arrived, Alex jumped out of the van and ran to me. He looked at me with his big eyes and said, "Nana, when can we go to Old MacDonald's Farm?"

Saturday morning arrived, and we were on our way. As we walked into the building to buy our tickets, Alex spotted a box on the floor. The box was full of swords of every color, size, and shape—and I could see Alex wanted one. I said to him what every good Nana says, "Alex, if you are a good boy today, I will buy you a sword when we are done." He was perfectly behaved all day.

When our excursion was over, he ran to the sword box, and I could see his little eyes darting back and forth between his two favorites—from the blue sword to the white one. He simply could not decide. One moment it was the blue one, the next moment it was the white one, until he finally said, "Okay, Nana, I'll take the blue one." We made the purchase and headed to the parking lot.

We had not even arrived at the car when he tugged at my hand and said, "Nana, I really want the *white* one." Too late. The blue one had been purchased. He cried all the way home, but even though it broke my heart, I felt he needed to learn early in life the results of making choices.

It was a whole year later that we were visiting his family on Vancouver Island, British Columbia, when I asked Alex if he would like to come along with me to run an errand. I strapped him into his car seat, and as we were driving down the highway, I heard his little voice shyly admit, "Nana, I really wanted the *white* one!" Our eyes met in the rearview mirror, and I had to look away because tears were welling up in my eyes. If he would have demanded the white sword and whined, it would have been a different story, but what I really heard him saying was, "Nana, you did not hear what was in my heart."

I quietly responded, "Alex, I am so sorry you did not get your white sword."

Many months passed, and I was in the middle of my Christmas shopping when I saw it. A white sword. The most beautiful white sword I had ever seen. It had gold edging, gold tassels, and it had its own case. I bought the sword, took it home, and wrapped it up tenderly for my little Alex. I mailed it in a box with a note for his mommy to please put it under the Christmas tree so Alex could have it on Christmas morning.

I could hardly wait for the report. On Christmas morning his little blue eyes flew wide open as he saw that strange shape under the tree. Between ripping wrapping paper and unabashed giggles, he shouted over and over, "It's my white sword! It's my white sword!" Even at his young age he knew that this gift was not from Santa, but from his Nana.

I wanted him to have his magical, white sword. He never demanded it, but in his quiet way he told me the desires of his heart. I wanted him to know his request was significant enough for me to hear.

My love for Alex is a lot like God's love for me. He knows the desires of my heart, and he's just waiting for me to ask so he can grant them.

And how bold and free we then become in his presence, freely asking according to his will, sure that he's listening. And if we're confident that he's listening, we know that what we've asked for is as good as ours.

I JOHN 5:14–15 MSG

Cheez Whiz

– Gracie Malone –

The happiness of life is made up of minute
fractions–the little soon-forgotten
charities of a kiss or smile,
a kind look, a heartfelt compliment.

Samuel Taylor Coleridge, from "The Friend. The Improvisatore"

Joe and I, along with our teenage son Jason, had decided to spend Christmas with our son Mike and his family at their house in The Woodlands. It was a break with tradition, but one that would have its own unique charm. Relieved of the duties of being Home Management Specialist in Charge, I was free to enjoy my grandchildren on their own turf. Montana and Myles and I spent hours playing games, telling stories, and watching Christmas videos.

One evening I gathered the boys on my lap for story time. I had brushed my teeth, showered, dressed in comfy pajamas, and applied a liberal amount of anti-wrinkle cream (rather expensive anti-wrinkle cream, I might add!) to my freshly cleansed face before meeting them on the sofa.

I'd no sooner settled into the plush cushions when Myles

climbed onto my lap and hugged me tightly. The little guy's bright-blue eyes danced as he took my face in his hands in a gentle caress. Then he patted me softly on both cheeks and whispered, "Mmm, mmm, Gamma Gacie, you smell good!" He flashed a big grin and added, "You smell just like a piece of cheese."

I burst out laughing, until the startled look on Myles' upturned face stopped me cold. He grinned and sweetly added, "I *wuv* cheese!"

My heart filled with joy as I pulled the little boy close. What greater compliment could he have given? To him, I smelled good enough to eat!

The next morning, we awoke to discover a room full of toys for the kids and a few gifts for their grandma as well. The chaos of gift-giving and gift-receiving must have lasted an hour or so before I opened a gift from our son Jason.

As I removed the cellophane wrapper, I discovered a beautiful tray made of amber stained glass. Mounted on the tray was an assortment of bath-and-body products labeled "Aroma Therapy." I found myself wondering what actual therapeutic effect an "aroma" could have on a person. What kind of smell could alter my mood?

Reading from the label, I saw that Jason had selected "orange ginger." I couldn't wait to give the lotion the sniff test. It smelled good! Strong citrus overtones with just a hint of pungent ginger.

The next day, after a long drive back home, I gave the

products a thorough analysis. I soaked my body in a tub of hot water seasoned with bubble bath, scrubbed my feet with granulated gel, and anointed my skin with lotion. Later, as I settled under the blankets on my bed, I realized the products had indeed lived up to their therapeutic claims. I was completely relaxed, without a care in the world.

Except maybe for one.

I kept wondering if Myles would be equally enamored with a grandmother who smelled like a piece of fruit instead of his favorite cheese.

As I drifted off to sleep, the scent of orange ginger wafted up to my nostrils and my thoughts took on a heavenly perspective. I remembered something written long before high-tech sales gimmicks and media hype influenced our fragrance choices—words that describe an "aromatherapy" of the spirit. Seems there is one fragrance that cannot only warm a person's heart, it can literally change the world—the most fragrant and harmonizing aroma of Christ.

*Thanks be to God, who in Christ always leads us
in triumphal procession, and through us spreads the
fragrance of the knowledge of him everywhere.
For we are the aroma of Christ to God
among those who are being saved.*

2 CORINTHIANS 2:14–15 ESV

Through the Eyes of Grace

— Debi Stack —

Love is a fruit in season at all times
and within reach of every hand.

Mother Teresa, from Love: A Fruit Always in Season

I don't know which was heavier—the ripped grocery sack that held all my end-of-fifth-grade stuff or my heart that held another day's worth of cruel words from my classmates. Shuffling off the school bus as it stopped at my house, I resigned myself to another miserable afternoon and a long, lonely summer.

Just then, a familiar sound changed everything. From my front porch rang a cheery greeting: "There's our girl!"

I looked up, then ran—grinning—to the open arms of Grandma Grace. Tall and well-groomed, Grandma Grace had a natural aristocratic air that matched her regal profile. But her grand exterior belied her most endearing qualities—down-to-earth faith, an affectionate nature, and constant good humor. A beloved family friend since before I was born, she sometimes stayed with me while my parents worked. We adored her.

Aptly named, Grace Darling had a joyful outlook on life. It sparkled from her eyes; it shone in her smile; it seasoned her speech with genuine kindness. This was a woman who created reasons to celebrate. Who else would phone us out of the blue to say, "I just paid my bills—let's have a picnic!" She maintained her deportment even while teaching me—between bouts of laughter—how to rise from lying on the floor with a cup of water balanced on my forehead. But on this day, because I had been expecting to enter an empty house, her presence especially delighted me.

"Come on in. Don't you look pretty? How about a treat?" Grandma Grace hugged me tightly, then led the way to the kitchen. I leaned against the counter next to her, mesmerized at how she peeled an enormous apple with a single, springy strip. After quartering and seeding it, she sliced ... and sliced ... and sliced ... until no slice could possibly be sliced again.

At last, paper-thin pieces of succulent apple towered in my bowl. Lifting it to the kitchen window and turning it slowly, I watched the color-changing play of sunlight upon the translucent slices—snowy white, cool ivory, flawless cream, or the palest glowing gold I'd ever seen. Yes, these were the same apples that I chomped right out of my hand on most days, but somehow, when Grandma Grace prepared them, they tasted like a delicacy fit for a princess.

Maybe that's because as she sliced the apple, Grandma Grace visited with me as if I were the most fascinating person in the world. She *looked* at me when I talked—always smiling—and never failed to interject generous compliments. When I groaned that boys didn't like tall, brainy girls like me, she replied, "But haven't you noticed that all the Miss Americas are tall and smart like you? You could be Miss America someday!"

Since then, apples have always reminded me of Grandma Grace. In her hands, this simple snack became something extraordinary. The glistening crescents of fruit that filled my empty bowl—slice after slice after slice—showed I was *worth* the extra effort. But sweeter still were the simple words from Grandma Grace herself—word after word after word that filled my aching heart:

"You are beautiful."

"You are special."

"You are talented."

"You are important."

"You are loved."

Grandma Grace passed away soon after I graduated from college, but during the lonely years of my girlhood, and even through some of the hard times in my adult life, I have often recalled her spirit-nourishing words. Time has not lessened their sweetness, nor is my heart ever filled to less than overflowing.

A word fitly spoken is like apples
of gold in a setting of silver.

PROVERBS 25:11 ESV

Connecting Around the Globe
— Gracie Malone —

Absence makes the heart grow fonder.

Unknown

Our youngest son, Jason, was over forty before he found the love of his life and began talking about marriage and having children. "Mom, tighten your seat belt, this is going to happen fast—we want to have babies, at least two, close together. I've wasted enough time already!" I was uncontrollably happy, wanting to float a few questions, but trying hard not to spoil the moment.

If you are a grandmother, you understand what I *did* say. "I can love as many as you can put through school!" You can probably also understand what I *didn't* say. Thoughts backed up in my mind like traffic on a Dallas-Fort Worth freeway. *And buy clothes and cars and houses and furniture and ... food ... and ...! Stop it, Gracie!*

Jason gave me a minute to breathe, then continued. Like lots of people, he had "found" the love of his life at the office—only difference was, the office was in Indonesia. Jason worked there on an international assignment for a Houston oil company. Another factor, one I didn't yet know, was that Jason had signed on for an extension to his contract.

As for the compatibility factor, Jason spoke the truth—the two of them held the same position in the company, same education, same religion, same likes and dislikes, and the same passion for life, love, and parenthood. He showed me a picture of them running stairs in the Indonesian marketplace. Same T-shirt and shorts, same sweaty brow, same big grin. Junipa, with her stunning olive skin and flashing brown eyes, was not only compatible but beautiful inside and out. I was convinced. They were a perfect match.

Within a year Junipa and Jason were married and had blessed us with a tiny baby girl, Zoe Sofia. Fifteen months later they introduced us to Mia Grace. It was then they called a family conference. Jason had been asked to manage a project in Saudi Arabia, and just like that, our children and grandchildren were packing for a trip to the other side of the world—*the other side of the whole wide world.*

If it is six o'clock in the morning here, it's six in the evening there. If I am going to sleep, my grands are waking up. If I'm eating breakfast, they are getting ready for bed.

One morning as I pondered their departure, I grabbed Papa Joe's hand, opened the Bible, and found this verse: "Before I formed you ... I knew you; before you were born I set you apart" (Jeremiah 1:5; also see Galatians 1:15). The long-distance relationship between grandma and grand-girls had been planted in the fertile soil of a divine plan. If our heavenly Father was in control, how could I mess things up? Did I even want to try to change things? I breathed a prayer and knew. I would shake off my wee bit of reservation, accept the choice, and apply some long-distance grandmothering!

Sure enough, Zoe and Mia have grown like weeds in the garden. Just the other day as we were connecting on our three individual iPads, six-year-old Zoe took advantage of a brief silence and began to sing a lyric about God making a way where there is no way. Her gentle voice reverberated in the space around my chair, lifting my heart and a burden that I didn't even know was there.

Then Mia ran into the room shouting, "Grandma! I love you six million." *Six million what?* I wondered for about one second and then knew: six million of no-matter-what would be enough for today.

God can pour on the blessings in astonishing ways
so that you're ready for anything and everything,
more than just ready to do what needs to be done.

2 CORINTHIANS 9:8 MSG

Grandma's Matchmaking Service

– Bonnie Afman Emmorey –

Two of my grandsons were playing marbles
when a pretty little girl walked by. "I'll tell you,"
said Jake to J.D., "when I stop hating girls,
that's the one I'm going to stop hating first."

Encyclopedia of Humor

Coming from a family of true romantics, I shouldn't have been surprised—but I was. My oldest son, Nathan, a college student, wanted me to be his matchmaker. In fact, when I would return from ministry trips, he would phone to ask if I had met any interesting young women he should meet.

I set him up with intriguing and fun email correspondences with lovely candidates from across the country, including a beauty queen, a professional singer, a chalk artist, and several dynamic and captivating university students. Many friendships developed, and I felt that any one of these women would have fit very nicely into our family. But somehow nothing more came of my "setups."

My son's godly grandma, my own mother, had been praying for both my sons' future wives since before they were born. In fact, Mother called me often, inquiring about their current love interests. So when Nathan called Grandma and also asked her to be a "matchmaker," I don't think she was surprised at all.

Nathan had noticed some very attractive and fascinating young women at Grandma and Grandpa's church and decided that Grandma was the perfect go-between. Knowing she is a wonderful cook and that hospitality is her gift, he asked her to check on the availability of potential blind dates and to feel free to set up a dinner engagement for him.

My mother was born for a job like this. She did the research and made the calls. She found an appropriate prospect and set up the date. She cooked a delicious meal, and everything was perfect—including dessert. Of course, I had to call when, after a few hours went by, I hadn't heard a thing. The suspense was killing me! Mother answered the phone and let me know that everything was fine. "The kids" were taking a stroll down their picturesque country road after dinner. She said the conversation at the dinner table had flowed easily, and she was quite pleased with her matchmaking. She was sure Nathan would call me later. He did just that and told me he had a very enjoyable evening.

My mind went back to earlier years. Nathan had grown up hearing stories of Grandma and Grandpa's romantic love story. It was considerably better than most books or movies. Both of my parents were engaged to someone else when they met, but that didn't stop Grandpa from knowing a good thing when he saw it. It wasn't long before they both knew they were meant for each other, and then the excitement really started.

They eloped—and kept their marriage a secret for a full month. Grandma's dramatic love story is one of Nathan's favorites. In fact, he has been known to use it for the entertainment portion of his own dates. You may have already guessed he has also inherited his grandmother's storytelling.

That blind date was neither the first nor the last of Nathan's dates at Grandma's house. He loves her cooking, her prayers, and her tolerance of his teasing, but he especially appreciates her interest in matchmaking. So far, the effort has not produced a permanent result—but it has challenged her to continue to pray that her grandsons find Christian spouses who will pass along a legacy of faith to future generations.

She is clothed with strength and dignity;
she can laugh at the days to come.
She speaks with wisdom,
and faithful instruction is on her tongue.

PROVERBS 31:25–26

Technically Speaking

— Gracie Malone —

*I'm not sure if life is passing me
by or trying to run me over!*

Plaque in my office

I was still in la-la land when I heard a heavenly-sounding Christmas carol coming from my cell phone beside the bed. I checked my pulse. Yep, I was alive! My heart was beating a bit too fast, but my mind was catching up. I remembered I had installed a "Carol of the Bells" ringtone last night. Christmas was coming and somebody was calling. I lifted the phone to my face, got a glimpse of five-year-old Zoe on FaceTime, and mumbled, "Good morning, sweetheart."

"It's not morning, Grandma Gracie! It's evening. Don't you remember?" Of course I remembered, and I reminded her that it *was* morning from my perspective. With my son working for a Houston oil company at an office in Indonesia, our time zone differences were major.

It had become a game with Zoe, a funny routine where I forget what time it is. This happened regularly, bringing a bit of fun to my mornings, or to my evenings—or whenever.

"It's not morning, Grandma, it's evening!"

"Are you sure, Zoe? I see the sun coming up!"

After a similar exchange Zoe politely asked, "Grandma, do you know about a.m. and p.m.?"

But on this day, Zoe giggled and introduced me to her new stuffed toy. He reminded me a bit of the Raggedy Andy that once-upon-a-time lived at our house in the US. "His name is Foxy, and Grandma—he lives in a box." She turned him upside down, box and all, and added, "Oops, I've got to change a diaper!"

And so it goes—grandma and grandchild making the most of a long-distance relationship using long-distant toys that miraculously work efficiently on very long-distant waves of air— I think.

Those two little granddaughters, Zoe, six, and Mia, four, have charmed me to the core with their delightful personalities and the simple fact that they *want* to chat with me. Technology makes this happen. It's a blessing beyond big! Were it not for iPads, iPhones, and laptops, I would hardly even *know* my grands! And they would not know certain valuable facts about their dad. They are delighted to hear stories about him.

After learning that *their* daddy was *my* son, the internet hummed pathetically as they told me a few stories too. One day I noticed a message from Zoe's iPad. "Grandma Gracie," she began, "I need to tell you about *your son*! Can I write anything that I want to? It's a secret."

What was I to say? "Of course you can. What's up?"

"Well, he thumped me on the head," she laughed. But later when I questioned Jason's thumping, she giggled. "Grandma, Daddy was just playing; it's funny."

On another occasion Zoe sent the following text: "Grandma Gracie, your son made me cranky."

I stifled a laugh as I pecked out a reply. "Whaaat? How did that happen?"

Zoe clarified with an altogether charming solution, "No worries, I told him what he did was wrong." She had indeed! Jason said she had texted him, "Daddy, this morning you made me cranky. You need to do better at wake-up!"

Must be easy and fun for my precious grandgirls to have a daddy, my son, who plays and hugs with the same degree of gusto that accompanies his patient correction and discipline. I know from experience this is not the norm, even in most Christian homes. What a pity, when Jesus Himself told us, and presented a pattern for, the way we should handle the little ones that live in our midst.

> "Allow the children to come to Me; do not forbid them,
> for the kingdom of God belongs to such as these.
> Truly I say to you, whoever does not receive the
> kingdom of God like a child will not enter it at all."
>
> MARK 10:14-15 NASB

The Birthday Gift

— Ginger Shaw —

Kids are smart, you know, and they know what's going on. You're not fooling them a bit. They know you're bewildered and confused and don't know all the answers, and they know that the louder you say something the less sure you are that it is right.

Bob Benson

The package arrived in time for my thirteenth birthday. Small and simply wrapped, it was sent from Nana, my paternal grandmother in California. We seldom saw Nana or heard from her, but she always sent birthday and Christmas gifts. And she gave great gifts. Not expensive, not fun toys, but real "lady" gifts: fancy stockings, grown-up gloves, and beautiful things. As I removed the brown paper and flowered wrapping tissue, my eyes fell upon a small, elegant white-leather Bible with my name embossed in gold on the front cover—just like the one my older sister received on her thirteenth birthday. The gift made me feel mature.

I knew this was an important gift, a real coming-of-age present. What I didn't understand was why Nana sent it.

I had never seen her go to church, never heard her talk about God nor heard her mention any story from that book. Oh, there was a large, old Bible on a table in her living room. But, with the exception of births and marriages written in the front, it appeared unread, unused, and untouched. And the few times I ventured to look inside that book, I was reminded it was to be left untouched.

I had missed growing up around my grandmothers and had never known my grandfathers. I do remember visiting my maternal grandmother and walking to church with her on Sunday mornings while most of the family slept. I remember, too, talking with her about all the stories I'd heard in Sunday school and church. Her simple answers, kind nature, and gentle wisdom taught me much of what it meant to be a Christian. That was the year that I experienced a personal relationship with God through faith in Jesus Christ. It meant a lot to me.

But I have never understood what faith meant to my paternal grandmother—my Nana. I've wondered if she simply thought of faith as a religious tradition. We lived 3,000 miles away from Nana, so I couldn't ask her in person why she sent me the Bible. And I'm not sure I would have asked her. Not once do I remember her sharing a personal memory or story. Perhaps it was just her generation or her personality. Nana didn't talk about herself; she gave instruction and correction. So instead, I sent the obligatory thank-you note.

Over the years I continued to wonder about the meaning of that gift and tried to understand this woman I never really knew. I excused her closed personality as due to distance, circumstances, or past pain. But then I thought of my other grandmother, who leaped tall mountains to be with us whenever possible. She opened her heart and mind and let me look inside the pages of her life. She and I are both richer for her openness.

In retrospect, both of my grandmothers taught me the same lesson: you really *can't* tell a book by its cover. It is the life lived as an open book that is the greater gift. I intend to live an "open-book life" and leave the story of God's work in my life for future generations.

You yourselves are our letter, written on our hearts,
known and read by everyone. You show that you
are a letter from Christ, the result of our ministry,
written not with ink but with the Spirit of the living God,
not on tablets of stone but on tablets of human hearts.

2 CORINTHIANS 3:2–3

Grandkid Quips and Quotes

— Gracie Malone —

Lettin' the cat outta the bag is a
whole lot easier 'n puttin' it back in.

Will Rogers

One bright morning, an aged grandfather and his four-year-old granddaughter were sitting on the front porch talking. As children her age are prone to do, she began probing him with questions.

"Did God make you, Grandpa?"

"Of course God made me," the grandfather answered.

After a moment, the child said, "Did God make me too?"

"He sure did," the man answered. He couldn't hold back a proud grin as he looked into her bright, blue eyes and saw her tiny legs twirling in circles as they dangled from the too-tall wicker chair.

For several minutes, the little girl seemed to be studying her grandpa as well as her own reflection in the window. He wondered what was running through her mind. At last, she spoke up, "You know, Grandpa, God's doing a lot better job lately."

***

Our son Mike and his buddy Tommy were both four when their curious little minds got them into a heap of trouble. All day long they'd watched from Tommy's backyard as movers unloaded a huge van parked in front of the vacant house next door. As the men tugged on furniture and rolled appliances into the house, Tommy and Mike became more and more curious about the new neighbors. Finally, a friendly-looking lady came out the back door. The boys jumped out of the sandbox and ran to the chain-link fence that separated the backyards. In typical preschool fashion, they struck up a conversation.

"What's your name?" Tommy began.

The lady smiled. "I'm Mrs. Frawley."

Like two kid-sized lawyers they put their heads together for a small conference. Then Tommy took a deep breath and fired off another question—the most important question of all.

"Do you have any little boys in the house?"

"No," Mrs. Frawley answered.

The boys were visibly disappointed. Nevertheless, after a moment, Mike continued the inquisition where Tommy left off. "Do you have any little girls in the house?"

"No, I don't," she answered patiently.

Tommy turned his hands, palms up, looked at Mike, then back to Mrs. Frawley. "Do you have a baby in the house?"

"No!" Looking a bit perturbed, the new neighbor turned to go back inside.

By this time Tommy was completely frustrated. How could a mommy and daddy not have children? And, more specifically, how could the people moving in next door not have kids for Mike and him to play with? As Mrs. Frawley made her way toward her back door, he shouted, "Well, do you have any babies in your tummy?"

***

"Where do babies come from?" is one question that has universal interest for deep-thinking four-year-olds. And when the topic comes up, it causes many a mother or grandmother to catch her breath and pray for wisdom. The question surfaced at our house one day as I sat on the floor playing with our grandkids—five-year-old Mary Catherine and eight-year-old Connor.

Mary was rearranging the dress on her Barbie doll when, out of the blue, she said, "I don't know how a girl can have a baby when she's not married." I fumbled with a tiny pair of Barbie's high heels and waited, hoping one of her parents had overheard the conversation and would come to my rescue. No such luck. I was still trying to formulate an answer when Connor spoke up.

"Oh, Mary." He twisted his lips into a crooked smirk and quipped, "Don't you know anything? You adopt!"

*"I praise you, Father,
Lord of heaven and earth,
because you have hidden these
things from the wise and learned,
and revealed them to little children."*

MATTHEW 11:25

The Greatest Cheerleader
— Shari Minke —

Grandmas are moms with lots of frosting.

Unknown

"Mom!" my new stepson shouted. "Grandma wants to talk to you!"

Picking up the phone, I said, "Hi, Dorothy. How are you?"

"Fine, dear, and how are you doing?" I internalized that she called me *dear*.

After the usual small talk, I risked asking, "Dorothy, may I ask you a personal question?"

"Sure," she said spontaneously.

"Recently, I was talking with the mother of my friend Sandy. Sandy died of cancer, leaving two little boys behind, just like your daughter Nancy did. Sandy's mother, Betty, told me that when her son-in-law remarried, it was difficult for her to hear her grandsons call another woman *Mom*. Betty thought you may be having some of those same feelings. I never thought about how hard it might be for you when you hear Doug and Scott call me *Mom*. Is that painful for you?"

There was a pause. "Yes, dear, to be honest, it does hurt. But I want you to know it has nothing to do with you. What is painful is that Dad and I miss our Nancy, and we always will. Even though it hurts to hear the boys call you Mom, we wouldn't want it any other way. We love you, and we're glad you're the mother of our grandsons. We don't always understand God's plans, but we believe that now God wants you to be the mother of Doug and Scott."

Many months later, Dorothy told me, "Just before you and Tom were married, Dad and I intentionally moved to Florida to live for a few months, hoping the boys would bond more quickly to you if we weren't around."

The love and sacrifice of these precious grandparents was astounding!

While Grandma and Grandpa were in Florida, every two weeks on Sunday morning, the boys ran to the phone to talk with them. Earlier when their daughter Nancy was fighting her battle with leukemia, they had been the primary caregivers to their grandsons. This resulted in a very close relationship between the boys and Nancy's parents. Doug and Scott smothered Grandma and Grandpa with hugs and kisses when they arrived back in Michigan to live.

At any of Doug and Scott's sports activities, Grandma rose to her full stature of four feet, ten inches, clapping and cheering, "Go, Scott! Go, Doug! Yea! Good job!" One warm summer night while sitting on the bleachers, Dorothy confided to me, "Before Nancy died, I promised that on her behalf I would yell the loudest for the boys to cheer them on." Tears welled up in my eyes.

As Mother's Day approached, my heart was filled with appreciation for this remarkable woman. In the letter I tucked in her card, I expressed these thoughts:

Dear Dorothy,

Without you and Lefty, there would have been no Nancy. Through your love, Nancy was born and blessed many lives, mine included.

In two days, our country will celebrate Mother's Day. I wanted to write you because I want you to know that in my heart, I honor you and Nancy. Two weeks ago, I was touched deeply that you introduced me as your "daughter-in-law." From the first time I met you, you have given me unconditional love and acceptance. You have always been an encourager and a support.

While I call you Dorothy to your face, in my heart I call you Mom.

I am thankful that you and I have been able to talk openly through the years. I thank you for cheering for the boys all these years on Nancy's behalf at the T-ball, soccer, baseball, football, and basketball games. Nancy would be so proud of you for keeping your promise to shout the loudest! Bless you for your commitment to her and the boys.

On this Mother's Day, I honor both you and Lefty for the excellent Jesus-focused lives you have lived. God is saying to you both, "Well done, good and faithful servants."

Shari

Love ... is not self-seeking ...
It always protects, always trusts,
always hopes, always perseveres.

1 CORINTHIANS 13:4–7

Overcoming "G-Force" and Other Free Falls

— Luke and Gracie Malone —

You know you're getting old when you get the same sensation from a rocking chair that you once got from a roller coaster.

Unknown

I don't know what possessed me to say yes. Perhaps I wanted to be considered the world's coolest grandma. Or maybe I did it to satisfy my curiosity. But I think I just wanted to prove something to myself. After all, who wants to think they're too old or out of shape to keep up with the youngsters, or too chicken to try something new?

Once the decision was made there was no turning back. I fell in line with my twelve-year-old grandson, Luke. We were going to ride "G-Force!" There were so many kids pressed into the narrow spaces set aside for the waiting lines, I couldn't have turned back if I'd wanted to. Besides, I was way too cool to admit I was scared spit-less. As we waited, I tried to maintain a calm outward appearance even though my aging knees were knocking uncontrollably and my insides were in a knot.

The following is Luke's version of what happened

***

"Since my grandmother is always telling stories about me, it's my turn to tell one about her. Once around Christmastime, my dad's company had a party, which included a trip to Six Flags Over Texas. When we all got inside the park, we decided to get into separate groups and do our own thing.

"I challenged Grandma Gracie to ride the G-Force with me. It's like an elevator with seats inside. It goes straight up over a hundred feet, then plummets to the ground fast enough to put your stomach in your mouth. Although nervous, Grandma Gracie accepted my offer. We had to wait in line for almost an hour, and the whole time I was telling her stories about how fast and scary the ride was.

"They buckled us in, and we started our climb toward the top. Grandma Gracie braced herself by pushing against the front of the elevator with her tennis shoes. Of course, I was reassuring her the whole time by saying how the cars don't come off the track that often, and as far as I knew, nobody had ever died on this ride.

"We inched forward and upward slowly until suddenly the car stopped, lurched forward, and I saw a look of sheer terror cross my grandma's face. Then we dropped at a blindingly fast speed. Before we knew it, we were on the ground. Although the ride was quick, it still rattled my grandma pretty bad. Shaking knees and all, she hobbled off the ride and headed for the ladies' room. I heard her mutter, 'So *that's* what g-force means.'"

***

Having overcome the force of gravity, I felt like "Grandma Invincible," for when the family got back together, I stood in line with the gang for two or three more gut-wrenching, heart-stopping rides.

Thankfully, before we left the park, I got to choose the last ride. The whole family joined me on my personal favorite—the carousel. Seated on the back of that horse, I breathed a prayer of thanksgiving, thankful for enough stamina to keep up with such a lively bunch of grandchildren and for the way they tried to entertain me! And grateful that my heavenly Father had worked overtime to keep me safe.

> "Do not fear, for I am with you;
> do not be dismayed, for I am your God.
> I will strengthen you and help you;
> I will uphold you with my righteous right hand."
>
> ISAIAH 41:10

Grandma to the Rescue!

– Carol Kent –

That's it! I'm calling Grandma!

Seen on a T-shirt worn by an eight-year-old

It happened at breakfast.

Our son was spending a few days with his grandparents in the Upper Peninsula of Michigan. He had enjoyed several fun-packed days of high adventure in the great outdoors. The woods on the property provided a creative outlet for his imaginative ideas, for finding hiding places and building forts, and for discovering a wide variety of northern Michigan wildlife. Deer grazed in the front yard and wild turkeys could be seen crossing the gravel road. Robins, blue jays, finches, and sparrows took turns resting on the railing of the rambling old deck as they helped themselves to Grandma's generous offerings of seeds, grain, and fresh water.

Everyone knows when you visit Grandma's house you eat well. She is a remarkable cook, and to this day she takes delight in pleasing the palates of her guests—no matter how young. Grandchildren are her favorites.

On the morning in question, Grandpa helped with the preparation of breakfast. He opened an old mason jar of canned prunes and carefully filled three cereal bowls with an ample helping. He then covered the wrinkled fruit with the prune juice left in the jar before placing the bowls at each place setting.

Jason was called for breakfast and sat down at the table. The three of them joined hands, and Grandpa asked the blessing in his deepest and most authoritative voice. Following the "Amen," it was time to eat. Grandma had prepared eggs (sunny-side up), farm-fresh sausage, and whole wheat toast. She also made breakfast potatoes that had been sliced and fried. And there were prunes—lots of prunes.

Jason dived into the eggs, sausage, potatoes, and toast, but he hadn't touched the prunes. Grandpa observed his reluctance to begin eating the brownish bowl of squishy fruit and announced, "Jason, if you want to keep your 'plumbing' working properly, you'll have to eat a few prunes in your lifetime. They're good for the constitution, and besides, we don't waste anything around here. Eat your prunes, son."

Jason loved his grandfather, and he had always been an obedient child. However, even the sight or smell of prunes caused his stomach to rumble. He gripped his spoon, picked up a prune, and placed it in his mouth. Gagging, he managed to get it down and spit the pit into his spoon. Again and again, he dipped the spoon into the bowl and repeated this procedure until the fruit finally disappeared.

Grandpa then said, "Jason, the juice is just as good for you as the prunes, so why don't you empty that bowl, son?"

Jason gazed up at his grandma with a pleading look of desperation while fighting the urge to regurgitate. Suddenly Grandma spoke up. "Clyde, I forgot to get the chicken out of the freezer in time to thaw for tonight's supper. Would you go downstairs and take care of that before I forget?"

Grandpa stood and went down the basement steps. At that moment, Grandma picked up Jason's bowl of prune juice, and without a word dumped it down the drain of the kitchen sink. Moving fast, she placed the empty bowl back in front of Jason.

Grandpa emerged from the basement, chicken in hand. Placing it on the counter, he looked over at Jason's empty bowl of prune juice and said, "Now that wasn't so bad after all, was it?"

Jason's eyes locked with Grandma's, and they shared a moment of relief, humor, and a never-to-be-forgotten, memory-making moment of reprieve. Grandma had rescued her grandson. The secret was theirs, and it bonded them forever.

Eventually Grandpa heard the true story of what happened that morning. Now, the entire family laughs out loud as the story is repeated, complete with a few exaggerations. One thing is certain. As we make our memories and share our stories, we weave laughter, connection, and meaning into the fiber of our relationships with the next generation.

A twinkle in the eye means joy in the heart.

PROVERBS 15:30 MSG

From the Heart

— Gracie Malone —

*You really shouldn't say "I love you"
unless you mean it. But if you mean it,
you should say it a lot. People forget.*

Anonymous eight-year-old

One day after school, five-year-old Montana gathered a few pieces of red construction paper, a lace paper doily, plastic scissors, and a handful of markers. Then he began working on what seemed a rather complicated project. Seated at the kitchen table, he cut and pasted, colored with the markers, and occasionally wiped his forehead with the back of his hand. Obviously, he was creating a valentine. His mother, Jeanna, tried to be inconspicuous as she observed, not wanting to spoil her child's surprise.

Finally, Montana completed the project and asked for an envelope. Jeanna located an unused card envelope and pretended not to notice as her son slipped his handmade expression of love inside. He picked up the black marker, then with a satisfied expression on his upturned face, sweetly asked, "Mom, how do you spell *Mrs. Wray*?"

Suddenly Jeanna understood the valentine was *not* for her, but for Montana's kindergarten teacher. A flush of emotion swept over her as she realized her son was growing up. The reality hit hard. Montana's world was enlarging to include other adults he respected—and loved.

On one hand, Jeanna was pleased about her son's social growth, especially when she thought about the child's sensitivity and thoughtfulness. But she also felt like she was losing something precious. She was no longer the exclusive source of her son's childhood training. Her thoughts took a leap forward, and she wondered if there would come a time when Montana would value his teacher's instruction more than his mother's. She also realized there would be other women in her little boy's life—some that he would love deeply.

Then, like watching a video on fast-forward, she imagined a scene that portrayed Montana as an independent, self-sufficient young man, and felt a deep gratitude.

Turning toward the window she brushed away a tear that had spilled over onto her cheek. Jeanna didn't want Montana to see this display of emotion.

But Montana had noticed! The lad jumped up from his place at the table and rushed to his mother's side. Putting his arms around her waist he hugged her tightly and said, "Mom, I love you more than anybody in the whole world."

Jeanna slipped her arms around her son's tiny shoulders. "I love you, too, sweetheart."

After a few moments of silence, Montana took a deep breath and spoke with amazing perception and depth. "Mom, you have my *real* heart. I'm just giving Mrs. Wray a copy."

When Jeanna told me this story, it reminded me that God, our heavenly parent, wants his children to love him wholeheartedly too. Sometimes the children of God get the wrong idea. We think we can divide up our affections like pieces of a pie, giving part of our heart to God and smaller segments to our other relationships and interests. In our human, businesslike minds we think that is equitable and fair.

But God is not pleased with only a part of our heart, even if he gets the biggest piece. He wants it *all*, along with *all* our soul, *all* our mind, and *all* our strength. It may seem like we'd have nothing left to share with others when we have given it all to him, but the amazing truth is that when we love God completely, our hearts grow and love multiplies. We are free to love others with the most beautiful, intimate, holy affection the world has ever known—love that's *a copy* of the devotion we have for him.

> God is love. When we take up permanent
> residence in a life of love, we live in God and
> God lives in us. This way, love has the run of
> the house, becomes at home and mature in us.
>
> I JOHN 4:17–18 MSG

Just Call Me "Mud"

— Cynthia Spell —

*Joy is a net of love by which
you can catch souls.*

Mother Teresa of Calcutta

If you are looking for the perfect "southern belle," you need look no further. Picture Scarlett O'Hara, from *Gone with the Wind,* in the twenty-first century, but blonde and five feet, six inches tall. A beautiful package, and yes, she just happens to be my mother.

Since I became an adult, people have asked, "Are you two sisters?" Sometimes for fun, we have told a little white lie, and in our Alabama drawl responded, "Why, yes, yes we are." Once we are alone again, we giggle like schoolgirls. It was my lifelong prayer to look like my mother, so the compliment thrilled me. My mother felt flattered that she looked young enough to be mistaken for my sister.

When I joyfully announced that I was going to make her a grandmother for the first time, she was elated. During the time I tried to choose the perfect name, my mother made a foreshadowing statement. "Cynthia, since you are the one doing all the work of having this baby, I think you should be able to name her Mud if you want to."

As the reality began to sink in for her, she worried about what name my unborn daughter should call *her*—a premature concern of course, but if you knew my sweet mother, you'd understand the dilemma she now faced.

"I don't want any of those fuddy-duddy, tired old grandmother names like Memaw or Nana," she told me. "I would like for Elisabeth to call me *Honey*." In reading back through my journals, I smile because I referred to her as *Honey* for the first eighteen months of my daughter's life. It seemed the perfect name to me, denoting sweetness and, of course, matching the color of my mother's hair.

Like most children though, Elisabeth had a mind of her own. Living in different states, we only saw my mother every three months. As soon as my daughter could talk, all bets were off on controlling her grandmother's name. Elisabeth would ask, "Who is *that*, Mommy?" My response was always, "She is my mother." So Elisabeth walked around the house repeating, "My mudder, my mudder." Thus, *Honey* turned into *Mudder*.

After Elisabeth could speak more clearly, she changed the name to *Mother*. My son, Christian, quickly latched on to the name. When we are all together, people look quizzically at us when they hear my children call her Mother. Explanations are always required at school when my children announce that their "Mother" is coming for a visit.

Only once has the child-given name created a real problem. Around the age of two, Elisabeth and I were leaving Birmingham after a family visit. As I carried her toward the plane, she began thrashing in my arms and screaming, "I want my Mother! I want my Mother!"

All eyes turned suspiciously on me as if I were kidnapping this child. As I boarded, I kept explaining, "This really is my daughter, she just calls her grandmother 'Mother.'" Sliding into my seat as quickly as possible, I pulled out a bag of M&Ms and began stuffing her full of her first chocolate. Thank goodness the chocolate calmed her down in the same way it does me. I relaxed and breathed a sigh of relief.

Fast-forward ten years to my third child, Mary Camille, who decided to change her grandmother's name once more. I am amazed to see how the endearing love of a grandchild can melt the heart of any unsuspecting grandmother. Unable to say Mother, she began calling her *Muddy*. My mother thinks this is just the cutest name in the whole world. Now who could have guessed that my sometimes "reserved" mother would ever joyfully embrace the name *Mud*?

Since that name change, I have realized how love can change any heart. We may start out with preconceived notions of how we will plan and control our own lives, but when unconditional love arrives, our hearts melt. We don't always see it coming, but one day the warmth of that gracious love changes us. And our hearts grow soft in response to God's consistent, unwavering, dependable love.

This is love: not that we loved God,
but that he loved us and sent his
Son as an atoning sacrifice for our sins.

1 JOHN 4:10

'Tis the Season

— Gracie Malone —

A man is at his finest
towards the finish of the year;
He is almost what he should be
when the Christmas season is here; ...
He is less a selfish creature
than at any other time;
When the Christmas spirit rules him
he comes close to the sublime.

Edgar A. Guest, from "At Christmas"

One Christmas Eve, the family gathered in our living room for the reading of a few traditional stories. I selected "A Visit from St. Nicholas ('Twas the Night Before Christmas)," and Joe read the story of Jesus' birth from the New Testament. Afterward, we hung our stockings on the mantel and the kids put out cookies and milk for Santa. Then their regular nighttime ritual began. When the first round of bathroom breaks and drinks of water was winding down, just as I thought the kids were "nestled all snug in their beds," Luke, four, remembered one more thing he wanted to do.

He padded down the hall, ran to the refrigerator, selected a juicy red apple from the crisper, and headed for the front door. As the door creaked on its hinges, he explained, "This is for Santa's reindeer." He carefully placed the fruit on the welcome mat on our front porch.

The next morning, in the excitement of opening gifts and rummaging through stockings stuffed to overflowing with goodies, the special treat for Santa's reindeer was forgotten. Then suddenly Luke remembered. He jumped up, leaping over crumpled paper and ribbons as he made his way to the front door. He dashed outside, then came bursting back in clutching a brownish, wrinkled apple core in his little fist. "Come here!" he shouted. "Everybody, come! Hurry!"

We stood in unison and pushed through the front door and went out onto the porch wondering what in the world we would see. Luke was beside himself, pointing toward the yard. "Look! Those are sled tracks in the grass!"

Sure enough, something very sled-like had cut deep ruts in our lawn. Several of the decorative lightbulbs that lined both sides of our sidewalk were crushed on the cement. It was a convincing scene. Obviously, Santa Claus had landed and then lifted off right from our front yard.

Grown-ups as well as all the grandchildren stood wide-eyed. Joe glanced in my direction, shrugged his shoulders, and turned his palms up. The kids jumped up and down in their footed pajamas. After a few minutes, the little ones and their parents made their way back inside. It was then that Joe and I noticed our neighbor who lived three houses away.

He was stumbling around in his pajamas and slippers, rearranging a wooden nativity scene that had graced his well-manicured lawn. When he saw us looking in his direction, he yelled, "Looks like somebody got a go-cart for Christmas." Then he repositioned Mary and Joseph in front of the manger, adjusted the baby Jesus in the hay, and picked up a stray lamb. All the while he was straightening things up, he was grumbling loudly, "Ran right through my nativity! I wish they'd stay out of my yard. Those kids are driving me crazy!"

As I watched my neighbor fuss and fume, I couldn't help but think that, like the infamous Scrooge, he needed a good, old-fashioned dose of Christmas spirit. The kind of spirit that sees the wonder and joy of the season instead of all the things out of sorts. Seems to me, he needed to see Christmas through the eyes of a child.

Shout for joy to God, all the earth!
Sing the glory of his name;
make his praise glorious.

PSALM 66:1–2

Driver's Education 101

— Judy Hampton —

Sometimes the heart sees what is invisible to the eye.
H. Jackson Brown Jr.

We'd just finished an incredible Thanksgiving meal, and we needed some time to work up an appetite for dessert. I asked my fourteen-year-old grandson, Brandon, if he'd like to go with me in the car.

"Sure. Where are we going, Grandma?"

"Oh, you'll see," I said with a grin as we got into my car.

"Grandma, where are we going?" he asked again.

"Well, it's such a beautiful day, I thought it would be a mighty fine time for you to learn how to drive a car."

Brandon shot me a look of wide-eyed glee as his jaw dropped. "Are you serious, Grandma? Does my mom know?"

"Yep, I asked her permission before we left."

His enthusiasm was obvious, and his questions continued. "Where are we going? Is it far?"

"I thought we'd go down to the church parking lot. It's probably empty today."

We chattered on as we drove the seemingly endless three

miles to the church. Sure enough, the lot was as empty as our hearts were full. "Are you ready?" I asked, knowing this was a silly question. My grandson had been ready to drive since he first stepped into his red-and-yellow Little Tikes toy car—the kind he had to propel with his feet.

I gave Brandon a few basic instructions to get him started: "Don't kill us and have a good time!" Laughing, he got into the driver's seat.

"Buckle up," I said.

He was trembling. "Oh, Grandma, I am so excited. Look at my hands, I'm shaking!"

I continued with clear instructions. "It's so easy, Brandon. Just put your foot on the brake, put the car in gear, and then release the brake and push on the gas pedal slowly."

He started off like a pro. Round and round we drove in the huge parking lot. I'd say we went around at least ten jillion times! Then he started weaving in and out of the light poles until I was dizzy.

"Be careful now." I laughed, wondering if the neighbors could see a white car weaving all over an empty parking lot. "Would you like to see if you can park?"

"No big deal, Grandma."

He pulled right between the white lines as I clapped and exclaimed, "Perfect job! Okay, now back out." Suddenly the car lurched forward onto the curb.

"Stop! Stop! You have it in drive!" I squealed. The tires screeched as he slammed on the brakes. We looked at each other and broke into uncontrollable laughter. It would not have been so funny had he driven through the doors of the church.

Brandon got out to check and see if he'd burned some rubber. Sure enough, he had. "Well, I guess I should have put it in reverse."

"Hey, it works for me!" I said as my heart left my throat. As I began to relax, I noticed something glinting in the sunlight. "What's that out in front of us on the ground up ahead?"

"I don't know, Grandma, I'll stop and see." Brandon put the car in park and walked over to an object lying on the ground. It turned out to be a silver-and-black leather bracelet, a cheap copy of a well-known brand. He brought it back and gave it to me.

"Here, Grandma," my grandson said. "I want you to have this bracelet. It's a present from me to you. It is my gift for taking me driving. I am having such a great time."

Accepting his thoughtful gift, I said, "Thank you so much, sweetheart."

After an hour or so of driving, he asked if he could use my cell phone. "Hello, Mom, guess where I am. I'm driving down the 57-freeway going ninety miles an hour in Grandma's car! Hope ya don't mind! We're heading to San Diego." I could hear her laughing. "Let me talk to Grandpa! Grandpa, I was driving Grandma's car down the freeway and hit a truck. Sure hope you don't mind." He giggled.

After the calls, Brandon turned to me. "Grandma, this has been the greatest Thanksgiving Day of my life. Thank you. I will never forget this day."

That did it—he's in the will. Oh, how I love this boy!

Finally, it was time to go home and have our dessert. When we reached his street, I asked, "Wanna drive the rest of the way home?"

"Yes-s-s-s!" he hissed. He jumped behind the wheel and drove up the street. He gingerly parked in front of his house and then leaned on the horn until all the family came out to cheer.

"Life doesn't get much better than this," I whispered as I got out of the car with a smile on my face. I knew that someday my grandson would be driving his own car. Someday a darling girl would probably be sitting next to him. Someday he might even give her a diamond ring. But today, well, today was a very special day indeed. I had gotten a date with my grandson—and had a silver bracelet to prove it!

A cheerful heart brings a smile to your face.

PROVERBS 15:13 MSG

"Wanna Play, Grandma?"

— Gracie Malone —

Part of being a champ is acting like a champ. You have to learn how to win and not run away when you lose.

Nancy Kerrigan

For most of us grandmas, there's nothing more enjoyable than playing with our grandkids, especially after we realize we're helping them grow socially and develop important skills. I've noticed how playing games has helped our little ones learn to listen and observe, as well as to follow directions and solve problems. Some games teach important concepts, like sportsmanship, and others provide valuable information.

Montana, our five-year-old, loves to play with his "Name the Animal" cards. He and his Grandma Gracie have been "naming the animals" since he was old enough to talk. The cards portray sixty-five different creatures identified in big block letters. On the back, there's information about the animal's characteristics and way of life. When I flash a card, Montana yells out the proper name. Sometimes we talk about the facts on the back of the card, but identifying the creature is counted a win. As Montana stacks up the cards he can identify, I "win" the ones he can't. Yeah, I know the cards are stacked against me. There's a fool born every minute, and in my house—for the sake of the kids—I keep being reborn.

Through the years, Montana has learned a lot about animals, and the cards have even helped him learn to read as he tries to sound out some of the names beneath the pictures. Besides that, as we've interacted with each other, I've had the sheer fun of seeing his sense of humor bloom like pansies opening to the morning sun. One day, I was flabbergasted when he couldn't identify the aardvark, and then he called the zebra a giraffe and the rhino an elephant. After he saw I was genuinely confused, he giggled and said, "I tricked you, Grandma Gracie! You thought I didn't know them!"

Not all the games we play provide usable data. Some are just-for-fun games that actually have very little redeeming value; others border on the ridiculous. In the latter category is another of Montana's favorites—a classic card game called Old Maid.

It's a simple game where players try to collect the most pairs by choosing randomly from their opponent's concealed hand. As you match pairs, you just can't help but identify with the funny characters. I love being Bertha the Ballerina, and Montana's favorite is Freddie the Fireman. But neither of us likes to get the Old Maid card.

If you end up with her, you're declared the Old Maid, and you lose the game. Montana hoots and hollers when I draw the dreaded card. I think it's because the Old Maid looks so, well, *grandmotherly*. She has a tight knot of gray hair pinned up with two knitting needles, and her wrinkled face is painted with circles of pink blush and a trace of red lipstick. Dressed in an old gray sweater with an afghan covering her lap, she sits slumped in her rocking chair.

"That's you!" Montana giggles as I plop the card face up on the table.

"That woman is definitely not me," I say.

Montana knows full well I'm not the rocking chair type. In fact, I take great pride in being off my rocker and into mischief and fun. Nevertheless, a verbal tug-of-war often takes place until one of us gives up and deals the cards again. Every time my grandkids and I get together, some game-playing madness occurs.

Recently, Mike, Jeanna, Montana, and Myles arrived for an overnight visit. I heard the back door open and glanced up as Montana rounded the corner into the living room where I was sitting on the sofa. When he realized I was talking on the phone, he stopped dead in his tracks and waited for me to push the off button. I couldn't wait to give my precious grandson a big hug.

As I wrapped my arms around him, his very first words were, "What do you wanna play?"

I couldn't hold back a giggle as I turned my palms up

and said, "Whatever!" Then I quickly added, "You pick the game, I'll get the cookies and milk."

I do not consider myself yet to have taken hold of it.
But one thing I do: Forgetting what is behind
and straining toward what is ahead, I press
on toward the goal to win the prize.

PHILIPPIANS 3:13–14

Choose to Be Happy

– Bonnie Afman Emmorey –

*The pursuit of happiness is a matter of choice ...
it is a positive attitude we choose to express.*

Charles R. Swindoll

Choose to be happy. That phrase rang in my ears after visiting my sister and her baby, Jason. As her son would start to tear up, Carol's soothing voice would say, "Choose to be happy."

What? Is it possible? Can you teach that concept? That incident happened long before I had my own children and now grandchildren.

I was fascinated by the idea that my own children and grandchildren could apply this principle. It wasn't until I saw it in action and realized the power of a positive outlook that I realized the need to rethink my own attitude about many things.

My beautiful, bright granddaughter Shira has a way of looking at things that puts me to shame. In Hebrew, her name means "my song," and that is a superb description of her personality. My son Jordan says Shira has never had a bad day.

That is not to say she hasn't shed some tears. I've been told she may cry the entire time it takes her to clean her room, but then the tears end, and life is good—no, *better* than good—*great*. Her attitude is not controlled long-term by her immediate circumstances.

Because she is smaller in size, Jordan and Michelle eagerly awaited the approval of the COVID vaccine for kids. They were afraid that Shira would not survive a bout with the vicious virus.

The day arrived, and both Shira and her older brother, Shane, got their shots. Shane complained loudly about the pain in his arm from the vaccination. But Shira's response rocked me. She said, "That's okay. I don't use that arm much anyway." For someone with such a tiny frame, I'm sure that shot was extremely painful, but she could ignore the discomfort and focus on the positive. Her other arm was fine.

Talk about choosing to be happy—I would have been the one complaining far louder than Shane. I was amazed at what I learned from Shira. She's confronted many challenges, and may continue to face them, but she knows how to *choose* to be happy. My life is made richer by knowing and loving this precious gift from God.

Shout for joy before the Lord, the King.

PSALM 98:6

Words: The Good, the Bad, and the Funny

— Gracie Malone —

*The sun looks down on nothing half so good as
a household laughing together over a meal.*

C.S. Lewis, from The Weight of Glory

One night my daughter-in-law Jeanna confided, "Gracie, I felt so bad about something that happened this morning. I heard a loud crash coming from the bathroom, followed by a bloodcurdling scream. I just knew Montana had broken an arm or cut himself. I ran as fast as I could to the bathroom. I didn't know what I would see when I rounded that corner."

"Oh, my goodness! What happened?"

"Well"—Jeanna took a deep breath—"when I got there, Montana was draped across the side of the bathtub with the shower curtain crumpled around him, and he was clutching a piece of broken plastic. You know that gadget that holds our shampoo and soap? Seems he'd been swinging on it like it was jungle gym. When it broke, he fell and landed on his back. Anyway, other than a bad bruise, he seems to be okay. But we were both so scared!"

"Well, accidents like that happen—especially with little boys like ours. Why do you feel bad about it? You know, mothers can't be everywhere."

"I know. It's just that, well, I didn't respond the way I wish I had." She paused. "Oh, Gracie, when I burst through that door and realized he was okay, I yelled so loud he stopped crying and his eyes bugged out. Besides that, I said a bad word."

I patted her on the leg sympathetically. "It's okay."

I wanted to tell her that Montana wouldn't remember what she'd said, but alas, I'd already heard the story from the perspective of said five-year-old.

"Grandma Gracie," Montana had whispered, "my mom said a bad word."

"Well, I'm sure she's sorry about that. You know, son, sometimes grown-ups make mistakes just like kids do. I know she feels bad. You need to forgive your mother."

He shrugged. "Yeah," adding something that made *my* eyes bug out, "Grandma Gracie, she said the f-word."

I felt my blood pressure rising as I thought, *this kid's way too young to know such a word exists.* But I had yet to hear the whole story.

Montana paused, ducked his head, and continued. "Grandma Gracie, do you know what the f-word is?"

"I think I do." I swallowed hard and asked, "Do you?"

"Yep!" He picked at a string on his jeans for several minutes. "I'll tell you what the f-word is if you promise not to go 'Aghhh!'"

I had to conceal a grin. This kid knows his grandma so well! Now, I ask you, all you grandmas, what would you have done?

Well, I made the promise—and braced myself! "Go ahead and tell me, Montana, what is the f-word?" Montana wiped his forehead and exhaled loudly. This kid really hated to tell on his mom. After a long pause, he cupped his hand around his mouth and in a subdued tone said, "assss!" I jumped up and hurried out of the room. I needed a place to gather my wits. Suddenly, I remembered that Montana was too young to spell. Why, he barely knew the alphabet! Apparently, he'd heard the phrase *f-word* somewhere and figured all bad words fit into the *F* category.

Later that evening, I decided it was time to tell his mother what Montana had said. Besides, it was too good a story to keep to myself. As we sat huddled on the sofa in front of the fire, we both laughed shamelessly, then launched into a long discussion about reactions and how to handle them.

"It's not easy to control what we say," I said, "especially when it comes to a knee-jerk reaction. I've mumbled a few 'bad words' myself at times."

"Well," Jeanna said, "if you didn't goof up now and then, I wouldn't love you so much." Then she said with a grin, "I think it's time I get off my *rear end* and go to bed."

We get it wrong nearly every time we open our mouths. If you could find someone whose speech was perfectly true, you'd have a perfect person, in perfect control of life.

JAMES 3:2 MSG

No Peas, Please!

— Jennie Afman Dimkoff —

Waste not, want not!

Unknown

The spoon loomed closer. At eye level now, it swam before my eyes. My stomach roiled as the smell of canned green peas assailed me. Bile rose in the back of my throat. Just as the grip of steely fingers fastened themselves around my chin, I woke with a start!

Relief flooded over me. It had been a dream. As I lay back and drew a tremulous breath, the reality of what prompted the nightmare came to me. She was coming tomorrow. Grandma Gertrude was coming for a whole week—and she always brought canned peas.

"Jennie Beth, wake up, honey! You'll be late for the bus. You have to eat your breakfast and put on your Halloween costume!" Mama's voice was too cheerful after a night filled with pea-green dreams, but I groggily dragged myself downstairs and then got caught up in the excitement of the day. Mama brushed my long hair and fitted a wide white band with a hand-stitched, red cross attached to the front.

"You are going to be the prettiest seven-year-old nurse at the party," she assured me with a kiss. Her huge stomach stood between us, and I rested my cheek against it.

"Will our baby come today, Mama?" I asked.

"I think maybe it will. Hurry now, or you and Carol will be late."

"Does Grandma have to come, Mama? I don't want her to be here!"

"Jennie! Don't say such a thing! Grandma is going to help us while I go to the hospital. You be a good girl and help with your little sisters. And make sure you eat everything Grandma puts on your plate. You know how much that means to her."

Swallowing back a fresh wave of nausea, I left for school, wishing I could be a real nurse and go to the hospital with Mama instead. At recess, I told my friend Clara that Grandma was coming. Her response amazed me. "You're so lucky. I wish my grandma could come today. Nana brings treats in her purse and reads me stories."

Her comments left me more depressed. We didn't have a nice name like Nana to call our grandma. In fact, I secretly referred to her as Grandma No-No because she never let us do anything fun—and the only treat she ever brought was canned peas.

On the ride home from school, a familiar car passed the bus with the driver honking and waving. Stopping at the next corner, our father got out and waved for the bus to stop. I'd never seen Daddy so excited. "It's a *boy*!" he shouted. "A *boy*!" Carol and I were allowed to leave the bus and ride the rest of the way home with our jubilant parent, who, after fathering four daughters, had been given a son that day.

Grandma Gertrude actually smiled when Daddy told her the news—especially after hearing that the boy would be called Ben, after her late husband and Daddy's father.

"There will finally be an Afman to carry on the family name," she said with a hint of approval and then abruptly tackled dinner preparations. I eyed the can of peas staring at me from the kitchen counter. It was standing on end, at exactly my height, and I knew Grandma No-No and I would be at the table an hour longer than any of the others once again, locked in a battle of wills until my plate was empty.

That night when Daddy got home from the hospital, we had a talk.

"Daddy, how come Grandma Gertrude is so mean?"

"I don't believe she thinks she's being mean at all."

"But she force-feeds me things I hate. She won't let me leave the table until the last bite is gone, and she won't let me do anything I want to do."

"Well, did you know that your Grandpa Ben died when I was only sixteen years old?" Daddy sighed. "To be honest, your grandpa had a drinking problem, Jennie, and he didn't provide for his wife and four children very well. Sometimes Grandma's canned peas were all we had for supper. Her life was hard, but she raised me and your aunts and uncle by herself. Will you try to be thankful for Grandma this week?"

The next day, I took a new look at Grandma Gertrude. Her severe black dress was still the same and her stockings continued to flatten long threads of hair against her unshaven legs. But I noticed something else too. She never wasted anything, and every action she took was for a purpose.

Many years have passed since that memorable week. Grandma Gertrude is in heaven now, along with both her daughters. I like to think of her there—loving God and learning to smile and to rest in his care. I learned some important lessons from her, like that vegetables are good for you, and to work hard, avoid waste, and not give up when life is difficult. And someday, when I'm a grandmother myself, to never, never, never visit my grandchildren bearing canned peas. I also hope Grandma Gertrude would be pleased that today I'm a published author with the name Afman in my title.

> *Listen to your father, who gave you life,*
> *and do not despise your [grand]*
> *mother when she is old.*
>
> PROVERBS 23:22

Betwixt Tweens and Teens

— Gracie Malone —

Hire a teen while he still knows everything.

Bumper sticker

I've got one thing to say about grandparenting teens. It's a lot more fun than parenting them. While their moms and dads are dealing with our grandkids' coming-of-age and handling all sorts of complicated issues, like curfews, cars, and companions, we grandmas are free to simply watch them grow—physically, spiritually, and emotionally. And sometimes we are asked for a bit of input.

Observing our two oldest grandsons develop from precocious kids into a presumptuous teen and a fun-loving "tween" has not only been enjoyable, it's been stimulating and more than a little refreshing. For example, I called one day to see if Luke (now a strapping fourteen-year-old) and his younger brother, Connor (twelve), could mow our lawn. Luke listened politely while I described the task at hand, including edging the sidewalk. I thought Connor could use the leaf blower, "whack" the weeds along the fence, and sweep the deck in our backyard. I finished my sales pitch with, "Since your job as soccer referee is now over, I thought you could make a little money to sock away for a rainy day."

Luke cleared his throat and, in a businesslike tone, replied, "Well, thanks for asking us to work for you. I'll talk to my people and get back to you in the morning."

I couldn't help but laugh as I hung up the phone. I imagined Luke, mercenary individual that he is, rubbing his palms together before sliding down the banister to the living room and landing smack in the middle of his "people" to discuss the new job opportunity.

A few days later, after Luke's people had given permission, he and Connor showed up for work. They did a super job taking care of our lawn for a modest fee and provided entertainment completely free of charge.

As Papa Joe helped Connor manage the complicated task of weed-whacking, I asked him about school. "Connor, I know it feels good for school to be out for the summer. By the way, how were your grades?"

"Great!" Connor quipped in his usual staccato manner. "I made A and B's."

Of course, he was hoping I wouldn't notice the missing plural ending on the A. I laughed as I thought, *Ahh, sweet freedom!* My grandma status leaves me completely free to enjoy Connor's cute personality and let his mom and dad decide whether or not "A and B's" are good enough.

When the lawn-mowing project was completed, the

four of us relaxed in our living room, sipping from bottles of AriZona Rx Stress tea and chatting about one of Luke's favorite topics—the current movies. "Papa Joe, we need to go see the new X-Men film. You want to go with us, Grandma Gracie?"

"No, Luke. As you know, I really don't enjoy action films." I shifted on the sofa and continued knowingly, "In fact, I just can't get into those creatures that morph from one thing to another. Give me a good, old-fashioned dose of reality, a film with a storyline and a touch of romance, and I'll be there!"

"Grandma Gracie, you need to try something different—you know, vary your viewing experiences, expand your repertoire. And it seems to me you don't know much about X-Men." Luke twisted his lips into a playful grin and added, "For one thing, they don't morph. They are mutants." He shrugged his shoulders and turned his palms up. "Mutants don't morph!"

"Mutants don't morph?" All four of us burst out laughing at the absurdity of our conversation.

After Luke and Connor went home, I recorded this newly discovered tidbit of information in my notebook so I wouldn't forget it. I now offer it to grandmothers everywhere—free of charge. For one never knows when such info might come in handy.

As your grandchildren morph (or mutate) from pre-adolescent tweens into full-fledged, key-carrying teens, there may be times when their choices are troublesome, their antics less than funny. Still, they need "people" who believe in them wholeheartedly and love them unconditionally. And, perhaps most importantly, they need people who will simply listen and laugh at their stories.

One generation commends
your works to another;
they tell of your mighty acts.

PSALM 145:4

Brown Sugar Sandwiches

— Vicki Tiede —

> One hundred years from now ...
> it will not matter what my bank account was,
> the sort of house I lived in, or the kind of car I drove.
> But the world may be different because
> I was important in the life of a [child].

Forest Witcraft

In 1949, when I was only two years old, twins were born into our family. My biological grandparents had passed away, so while my mother was in the hospital, I stayed with the elderly couple across the road. I knew them as Grandpa Art and Art's Mama.

Art's Mama was really his wife, but as a toddler I didn't understand the nuances of relationships and their titles. Art's Mama always wore a smile and a cotton dress with a full apron. She was kind and attentive and protected me from their scary pet boxer in a no-nonsense tone of voice. Everything I know about being a grandma to my six grandchildren I learned from Grandpa Art and Art's Mama.

When Mother went into labor, Dad walked me across

the road to Grandpa Art and Art's Mama's farm. When Grandpa Art saw me coming down the long driveway he called out, "Here comes My Sally!" That's what my "adopted" grandparents always called me—My Sally. That pet name was an assurance I was loved and cherished.

Mother had to stay in the hospital for a week after the birth of my twin sisters. I had never been away from her before. Grandpa Art and Art's Mama knew this might be scary for me, and they made every effort to make my visit comfortable.

That week I had a terrible cold. Art's Mama concocted a home remedy made with smelly goose grease, and Grandpa Art attempted to put it on my neck and wrap it with an old gray sock. I flat-out refused to put that ugly old thing around my neck. Grandpa Art bent down, looked into my eyes, and assured me, "It will make your cold go away." As they fastened that old wool sock around my neck, Grandpa encouraged me in his gravelly, German-accented voice that I loved, "That's My Sally." I wore that sock for two entire days and refused to let them take it off.

Art's Mama made a special bed for me on the couch while I stayed with them. In their old farmhouse, they slept upstairs—but not that week. Grandpa Art insisted, "I can't possibly leave My Sally alone." Art's Mama made a bed on the floor beside the couch and that's where they slept, never leaving my side. The next morning, I woke up in an unfamiliar place.

Before long, Art's Mama pulled me up to the kitchen table and poured me a cup of coffee. "We are gonna make this taste real good now," Grandpa Art promised as he loaded it with milk and sugar.

For me, the fun was more about stirring this sweet treat, licking the spoon when I finished, and spending time with Grandpa Art and Art's Mama than actually drinking the coffee.

Grandpa Art insisted, "No cuppa coffee's complete without open-faced brown sugar sandwiches."

With that declaration, my grandparents taught me how to use the back of my teaspoon to pat the crunchy brown sugar onto a slice of buttered bread "just so" in order to prevent the sugar from falling off before it reached my mouth. This became our daily routine. Art's Mama smiled and made me feel like I was the most special guest she'd ever had.

Grandpa Art always wore bib overalls. In the skinny front pocket, he always carried an Almond Joy candy bar—and I knew there were two small candy bars in that package. He'd tell me, "The best part about an Almond Joy is that there are always two—one for me and one for My Sally." Art's Mama would smile, and I noticed she took great delight in the fun I had with Grandpa Art.

During that special week of my two-year-old life, I was given a gift that would become my model for being a grandma. Communicating unconditional love and commitment to my grandchildren comes naturally as I call them by special pet names and when I get down on their level to look them in the eyes. When we share a "cuppa coffee" together, our hearts are filled to the brim. I have, however, discovered that too many brown sugar sandwiches mixed with caffeine isn't always the best diet—so we save that treat for special occasions.

One thing we agree on is that nothing is sweeter than sharing something treasured with someone you love. Most importantly, I learned that the greatest gift of all is to give your time and love to your grandchildren. Now, I pass on the legacy of Art's Mama to those I love.

My children, our love should
not be just words and talk;
it must be true love,
which shows itself in action.

I JOHN 3:18 GNT

Ho, Ho, Holidays

– Gracie Malone –

Then the Grinch thought of something he hadn't before!
"Maybe Christmas," he thought, "*doesn't* come from a store.
Maybe Christmas ... perhaps ... means a little bit more!"

Dr. Seuss, from How the Grinch Stole Christmas

I'd pictured a Norman Rockwell Christmas—one with the family decked out in red velvet dresses and crisp white shirts, dining on glazed, carved ham and steaming scalloped potatoes, Christmas tree lights sparkling in the background. But that day—Christmas, of all days—the water main broke.

Our oldest son, Matt, had no sooner arrived with his four kids than our son Mike's four-year-old Myles popped through our back door and announced, "Dere's waddah gushing from the middah of de dwiveway!" as his brother, Montana, stood nearby. Myles jumped up and down excitedly. "Lots of it—a big waddahfall wunning down the stweet. Come look evahbody!"

With that pronouncement, we all pushed through the door to see what was up. Sure enough, Myles had described the scene well. We had to find a way to stop the flow. Luke and twelve-year-old Connor climbed through the bushes in front looking for the shutoff while the older members of the family tried to find the key for the water meter box. We looked like a bunch of adrenalin-charged clowns racing around the yard and rummaging through tools in our garage. It took at least thirty minutes to get the "waddah" turned off, leaving us drenched and dirty.

Instead of red velvet dresses and crisp white shirts, we had men with mud on their jeans and kids with dirt and grass stuck to their tennis shoes standing in a circle in the Malones' kitchen. The Christmas ham and cheesy potatoes were cooling on the stove. And the vegetables, well, they were still in the freezer. My daughter-in-law Jeanna and I shot stricken glances at each other as reality sunk in. We had no running water—nary a drip from the faucets, not a drop to even make tea. As I turned toward the gang that included three sons, six grandkids, and one frazzled husband, I didn't know what else to do but turn my palms up, shrug my shoulders, and grin. "Well, folks, have some ham!"

Without a moment's hesitation, Luke took the carving knife in hand and began passing slices of meat speared on its tip to his dad, brother, and granddad. Before I could locate some paper plates and ask, "Potatoes anyone?" the room was filled with laughter and boisterous details of the crisis that had just unfolded.

Thus, we dined—well actually, we picnicked—most of

us standing around the kitchen as we planned how to survive the night. Thankfully I'd stocked our fridge with "designer" drinking water, and we had two gallons of spring water in the garage for hand-washing. Jeanna and Luke decided they could keep the commodes in usable condition by filling the tanks with water from the swimming pool. Their idea became a bucket brigade that lasted throughout the night.

With a workable plan in mind, we gathered around our tree, read the Christmas story from the Bible, opened gifts, devoured a plate of chocolate fudge, and finally settled into an assortment of cots and beds. As I drifted off to sleep, I lamented about what our family missed by having to celebrate this significant occasion in such a haphazard way.

I shouldn't have worried. The next day we located a compassionate plumber who mended our water line, and we shared a nice family breakfast. Afterward, I asked each person what they enjoyed most about our unique celebration. Jeanna loved our new, nine-foot tree, sparkling with a thousand tiny lights. The grandkids loved their new games and toys. The guys grunted, almost in unison, "Yum, that meat! Served on a knife."

When the giggles died down, little Myles jumped out of his chair and shouted, "Gamma Gacie, I just wuvved that waddah! *Whooosh!* All dat waddah was way cool!"

We all burst out laughing. Later, after my kids and the grandkids had climbed into their cars and departed, I sighed deeply as I recognized something important. Christmas, after all, isn't about glitz, glitter, and perfectionism. It's about love and laughter and the feeling of deep content that comes from simply being together and solving problems as a team. Now I'm wondering what kind of bonding experience I can come up with for next Christmas!

"I bring you good news that will
cause great joy for all the people.
Today in the town of David
a Savior has been born to you;
he is the Messiah, the Lord."

LUKE 2:10–11

The Pickle Party

– Carol Kent –

The best thing to spend on children is time.

Anonymous

The invitation was irresistible. An exclusive five-star hotel chain was launching a new business venture that involved selling timeshares. We received a too-good-to-be-true offer to stay for four nights in a deluxe condominium located in a swanky resort community. They advertised in-room Jacuzzi bathtubs, and the property had three pools, a golf course, tennis courts, and fine restaurants. The location was only a forty-five-minute drive from our grandchildren—and if we were willing to sit through a ninety-minute presentation on why we should buy into "this astoundingly reasonable opportunity of a lifetime," we could enjoy all the amenities for four days at a minuscule price. We set the dates and invited my sister Bonnie to join us, along with our two granddaughters.

Arriving at our "home away from home," we were delighted to discover the facility lived up to the description in the color brochure. Chelsea and Hannah squealed with delight as they tried to decide which of the three large pools they would try first. After swimming to their hearts' content, the girls went to the recreation building and played ping-pong, boccie, shuffleboard, and basketball. We were definitely getting our money's worth out of this adventure!

It didn't take eight-year-old Hannah long to investigate the Jacuzzi in the master suite. "Grammy," she exclaimed, "there's a bathtub big enough to be a pool right here in your bedroom! Let's go swimming in here!"

Hannah, Aunt Bonnie, and I donned our swimming suits and filled the tub with water and bubbles. Bonnie (my most frugal and financially disciplined sister) had made a trip to the Dollar Store earlier, where she had purchased a jar of dill pickles. We had no other treats, so we piled a plate full of pickles and took them with us to the tub.

Before long, conversation started to get deep—three women in a tub, leisurely discussing the challenges and complexities of life. I eagerly looked for a window of opportunity for a heart connection with my young Hannah. We decided to call our Jacuzzi outing "The Pickle Party," and we promptly took turns picking dill pickles off the plate as we chatted and munched our way through the next hour.

"Hannah," I said, "what's the best part of today?"

Her response was right on: "Talking to girls about being a woman is *definitely* the best part of today." Her older sister, Chelsea, had recently entered puberty, and this was of great fascination to Hannah.

We discussed her conflicts with her sister. "We just don't get along with each other," she stated dispassionately. "I think our personalities are too different, and besides, she's always getting me into trouble." I knew the part about *who* got *whom* into trouble could be debated, but I decided to move to "higher ground" in our conversation.

Aunt Bonnie said she was turning into a prune, so that left me alone with Hannah, where we could move into more intimate conversation. "How do you think I can help you best, Hannah?" I asked.

"Well," she said, admiring her image in the big mirror next to the tub, "I think you can teach me about how to be a good mom. And I'll need to learn how to do laundry and housework." Her mind was moving in many directions. "And if I have kids, I don't think I can have a job too. But *you* have a job, don't you, Grammy, and your kid is my Daddy." I could see the wheels turning in her brain. Big decisions. Major choices.

"Hannah," I said seriously, "Grammy's been praying for your future husband."

Her eyes grew big, and she laughed out loud. "It's too early to pray for my husband, Grammy. I'm just a kid."

As I piled her soapy hair on top of her head in a coiffure, I said, "It's never too early to pray about who you're going to marry. It's one of the most important decisions that you make in life."

"Well, that's not going to happen for a long time," she

stated emphatically, "but thanks for praying for me." Then, chomping down her sixth dill pickle, she abruptly added, "And you need to teach me how to handle high electric bills." With that final comment, she decided we had taken enough time for grown-up discussion, and it was time to dunk our heads in the water and play.

We made a memory that day—Grammy and Hannah—having a pickle party amongst talk of puberty, sibling rivalry, boys, and grown-up matters. And from this day forward, every time we bite into a dill pickle, we'll both remember the closeness we shared that day.

> *Point your [grand] kids in the right direction—*
> *when they're old they won't be lost.*
>
> PROVERBS 22:6 MSG

It's About Time

– Gracie Malone –

Happiness is as a butterfly,
which when pursued is always
just beyond your grasp, but which,
if you will sit down quietly,
may alight upon you.

Unknown

When my grandkids are visiting, I look for opportunities to hang out with them, even if only for a few minutes. It doesn't take much time to put my arm around their shoulders and observe their current model-building project or settle beside them on the sofa to watch an inning of a baseball game or part of a movie. When I make myself available, I often find they open up and talk about things important to them, such as problems they're having with friends or some of the challenges they face in school. This is how intimacy develops. As an added bonus, I hear some of the funniest stories I'll ever hear—tales that get passed down from one generation to the next.

One afternoon, I was determined to take a little time

out for meaningful interaction with our four-year-old grandson, Connor. I enticed him to sit beside me on the patio by offering him a box of apple juice and a couple of cookies. As he sipped the juice and munched on the sugary snack, I could tell he was lapsing into a pensive mood. (Little Connor is our deep thinker—a child whose personality, at least from his dad's point of view, causes him to view life from a perspective that's "a bit on the dark side.")

The quiet moments on our deck provided a perfect opportunity for Connor and me to share some "deep thoughts." After watching the wheels of his little brain spin silently for a few moments, I asked a question that members of my generation ask young ones all the time: "Connor, have you thought about what you want to be when you grow up?"

He gazed at the clouds, then turned to me and said, "I want to be a horse." A horse! Not a horseback rider. Not a cowboy. But a horse!

I stifled a giggle, knowing such an irreverent reaction would end our serious conversation. Instead, I cupped my hand under my chin, Freudian style, and repeated back his words. "Hmm, a horse, huh?"

"Yep! A horse."

There was no word of explanation—just a simple declaration that left me scratching my graying head in utter amazement. Then Connor jumped down from his chair and ran toward the swing in our big oak tree.

Later that night as I settled in my bed, my mind returned to the conversation with Connor. I wondered what in the world he was thinking. Then I got a visual picture of a sleek black stallion running through flowered meadows—muscles rippling, cool breezes blowing through his mane. I pictured him grazing in lush, green pastures, drinking from cool mountain streams. As I drifted off to sleep, I decided Connor had a really good idea.

There are some days I'd gladly trade places with a horse.

He makes me lie down in green pastures,
he leads me beside quiet waters,
he refreshes my soul.

PSALM 23:2–3

Spin the Bottle

— Diana Pintar —

*If you don't have a little bit of heartache,
how do you know when you're happy?*

Unknown

As empty nesters, my husband, Mike, and I lived a quiet and well-ordered life in our barely big-enough-for-two detached condominium. As is true of many life-changing circumstances, an unexpected phone call signaled the end of one season in our lives and the beginning of the next.

Barely intelligible through her sobbing, my daughter, Cori, cried, "Mom? We need your help!" Her marriage had ended. Without financial resources, she and her seven-month-old son, Carson, needed a place to live.

Mike and I moved over to make room for unexpected guests. The entire downstairs of our home, a walkout that previously accommodated our home office and library, became their new home. We squeezed the former contents of those rooms into our tiny guest room. We crammed baby food and baby bottles into our already overcrowded kitchen, and we purchased a high chair.

Next, we set some basic ground rules to safeguard our physical and emotional boundaries:

That chair is Mike's.

If that door is closed, it means, "Do not enter! Don't even knock!"

Take off your shoes when walking on the hardwood floors so you don't wake the baby.

Childproofing everything was our final priority. With tears in my eyes, I packed up my breakables and unsafe-ables and stored them in Styrofoam-filled boxes. We even hauled a battle-scarred table from our basement storage to replace our tipsy, and therefore hazardous, glass-topped coffee table. With adhesive strips, we attached ugly corner protectors to the table to guard against bumps and bruises. Duct tape became a necessary adornment as the tiny strips failed to hold up to inquisitive toddler fingers. With the addition of a playpen and toys, the transformation was complete. Our once-beautiful living room was now a far less attractive, but baby-friendly, environment.

Similar changes occurred throughout the whole house. Drawers and cupboard doors received childproof locks. Doorknob protectors barred access to "out-of-bounds" rooms to curious babies on the move—and to adults in a hurry. Feelings were easily hurt. As fall became winter, we began to feel slightly claustrophobic and displaced: Who sits in the big corner chair? Inanimate items took on a life of their own: "Have you seen the remote control?" Tension grew. "How old are these leftovers?" It was too close for comfort, for me. I began to withdraw, both physically (behind the now frequently closed door) and emotionally (present but not "present").

One Carson-filled evening changed my perspective. Now an active toddler, Carson zoomed about the house burning off his dinner. Up and down the hallway he ran. As he whizzed by me, I reached down, caught him, and "loved all over him" (which consisted of lots of loud kisses all over Carson's head, face, and neck.) Carson collapsed into a pile of giggles at my feet.

On his next round, he veered toward me as he neared, passing tantalizingly close, as if to say, "Get me again, Grandma!" I grabbed him and again "loved him all over." This time, we both giggled uncontrollably as I set him back on his feet.

Our laughter drew the attention of Mike and Cori, who joined our game. The three of us formed a gauntlet down the hallway. As Carson dashed past, each in turn grabbed him and, to his increasing delight, covered him with kisses.

The house rang with laughter. Tears poured down our cheeks. Out of breath, I sat on the floor. It was not long before Cori and Mike joined me there.

Our new positions forced Carson to modify his strategy. Instead of running past us, he ran directly at us, throwing himself into our arms to collect kisses. Finally, he simply stood in the center of the hallway and spun. When he came to a stop, he allowed his body to drop in the general direction of the person he faced at the end of his spin. He trusted us to catch him and "love him all over" when he fell our way.

"He's playing spin the bottle," Mike exclaimed, "but he's the bottle!"

Carson's contagious joy, unmarred by the difficult circumstances, was an example to me. I looked around the small circle of family on the hallway floor. For the first time in months, I didn't feel like it was too close for comfort" but, instead, simply "close."

Life often takes sudden and surprising turns. Happiness in difficult circumstances is a moment-by-moment decision. My grandson, Carson, is helping me to create moments of happiness every single day.

> *A happy heart is good medicine and*
> *a cheerful mind works healing.*
>
> PROVERBS 17:22 AMPC

In Giving We Receive

— Gracie Malone —

*I do not ask for any crown
But that which all may win
Nor seek to conquer any world
Except the one within.*

Louisa May Alcott, from "My Kingdom"

Our grandson Myles absolutely loved his pacifier. This affection ... *errr* ... this obsession lasted from a few moments after his birth until he was almost four years old. By two, the device had a name, "Nah Nah," and it seldom left our toddler's mouth. As the relationship between pacifier and pacified grew, Myles could actually do tricks with it. He'd look up, grin an impish grin, and with a quick flick of his tongue give Nah Nah a 360-degree spin without missing a beat in the sucking rhythm he had going. The antic was so cute that sometimes I'd yank the pacifier out of his mouth, turn it upside down, and stick it back in, just to see his performance.

Sometimes Myles would giggle, clamp his hand over his mouth, and run before I could get a good hold on the plastic ring. At other times, he'd tease back, tilting his chin upward, then, quick as a wink, snap his head around so the pacifier was beyond my reach. It was a catch-me-if-you-can-but-I-really-hope-you-can kind of deal—a competitive sport that provided entertainment for the whole family.

Throughout the course of its existence, Nah Nah not only pacified Myles' natural sucking impulses but comforted him through many a crisis and soothed more than a few anxious moments. At bedtime, the pacifier was Myles' best friend, his mama in absentia. To lose Nah Nah in the middle of the night could cause a major crisis. Myles would realize the pacifier was missing, sit bolt upright in bed, howl loudly, and crawl around under the covers or on the floor until he found it and slapped it back in place. No wonder Momma would come running to help him find it.

After one unsettling night, to ensure never having to experience another unpacified night, Jeanna purchased a spare. *Ahh*, she thought, *sweet sleep*! She thought! But Myles came up with another plan. He toddled toward bed with both pacifiers in tow—one solidly plugged in his mouth and the other clutched tightly in his chubby little hand. What bliss! A suckling child with two "suckers"!

The only problem was, Myles had a hard time knowing which pacifier he loved best. Even at night, he'd plug one in, then pop it out and sample the other. This double dose of fun worked well until Myles matured a bit and became embarrassed—especially when sporting the two Nah Nahs in public. People would actually stop and stare when he'd remove one from his mouth, dig in his pocket for the spare, pop it between his lips, and give it the 360 as he tucked the first one safely away.

Eventually, even Myles realized he had a problem. When Jeanna suggested it was time to give Nah Nah up, he was willing. One night, just before bedtime, they made a dramatic stop at the trash can in the kitchen. Myles stepped on the lever and ceremoniously tossed both pacifiers inside. He strutted toward bed wearing a very grown-up smile. But after a few minutes, Jeanna heard a commotion in the kitchen. She turned on the light, and there was Myles sitting on the floor picking through the garbage like a pint-sized wino. His lips were quivering.

Jeanna couldn't bear it. She located one Nah Nah, gave it a thorough washing, and put the child to bed, where he slept peacefully. After a few more attempts, Jeanna and Myles addressed the problem one more time. He tossed the remaining Nah Nah in the garbage can and left it there. For a full two weeks, the little guy hardly missed his former addiction. He was well on the way to a complete recovery when he became sick.

On the way home from the doctor's office, Myles whined and pulled on his ear as his temperature soared. When they stopped at Target to fill a prescription, Jeanna buckled him in the shopping cart and clipped down the aisle toward the pharmacy. Suddenly Myles let out a moan that stopped his concerned mother dead in her tracks. Glancing up, she spotted an enormous display of pacifiers of all shapes, sizes, and colors.

Myles tugged at the seat belt as he stretched toward the display. "Nahhhh, Nahhhh," he wailed. The moan came from the core of his tiny being. Then he dropped his feverish brow on the handle of the cart and wept. Yep, Jeanna bought one, opening it on the spot.

A few weeks later "the talk" resumed. "Myles, I've got an idea," Jeanna began. "I'm wondering if you'd like to give your Nah Nah to someone else. I'll bet there's a little boy or girl much younger than you who needs a pacifier. We could put it on the front porch and see if the tooth fairy will pick it up and deliver it to someone who really needs it."

That evening before bedtime, Jeanna located a nice gift box and stuffed it with colorful tissue. Myles gently placed Nah Nah in the folds of paper. They tied a ribbon around the box and carefully placed it on the porch. Myles strutted to bed.

Early the next morning, he ran to the porch to see what had happened. Lo and behold, the box was gone. Apparently the Nah Nah had been picked up and delivered to a needy child. Myles seemed genuinely pleased when he called me. "Gamma Gacie," he began in his very best toddler talk, "I gave Nah Nah away!" I could hear the excitement in his voice as he added, "Another little boy needed it more than me."

"I'm proud of you, Myles," I gushed. "You are so grown-up!"

Later, I found myself thinking about Myles' courage and determination. I really was proud of him! After all, it's hard for a person—even a well-seasoned grandmother like me—to give up things that are pleasurable. Seems there is a part of us—an unmanageable toddler-like part—that longs to acquire and hang on to things we don't really need.

In a moment of self-reflection, I thought about a few of my own "Nah Nahs," like the clothes rack at Talbots and the coffee shop where I drool over Caramel Macchiato Lattes. I took a deep breath and marched to my bedroom closet. I picked out several outfits to give to a needy friend and a pair of shoes for my sister. I thought about a friend who I'd invite to join me next time I visited the coffee shop.

Later as I settled into bed, I felt good. For I'd been reminded of one of life's important lessons. It truly is in giving that we receive.

I have stilled and quieted myself, just as
a small child is quiet with its mother.
Yes, like a weaned child is my soul within me.

PSALM 131:2 NLT

It's a Bonding Thing

— Phyllis Harmony —

*May the wonder of today
be that of a child.*

Phyllis Harmony

It was my first Grandparents' Day event. My five-year-old granddaughter, Aggie, was in kindergarten, and she excitedly invited me to this special celebration. I arrived early and was directed to the auditorium filled with giggles and smiling, searching faces. My little redhead jumped and waved to me from the steps where she stood with her classmates. Every grandparent was the proudest one in attendance, listening to songs and laughing spontaneously as our grandchildren swayed with the music.

We followed our little darlings to their classroom to admire various stations. One exhibited carefully printed numbers, another the alphabet, and a third was filled with family photos. Sweet little fingers pointed, and eager hands pulled their guests around the room.

As my first grandchild, Aggie got to choose the name I would be called. She chose "Ma." Not Nana or Memaw or Nonie or Grandma, just plain Ma. I love the name and adore the voices that say it.

Aggie was excited. "Ma, let's go find the picture story I did. You're gonna love it. It's about you and me together!" We found a ceiling-high, four-sided bulletin board at one end of the room. Aggie searched high and low for her picture. I could see that every paper had the words "Together we ..." printed across the top, followed by a picture and a one-sentence story of something they did with their grandparent.

With tears welling up in her twinkling brown eyes, she proclaimed, "I can't find it! Ma, it's not here, but I really did one, and it was good." Her voice trailed off in sadness and frustration. I started the grandparent search to assuage her disappointment. I looked way up to the top. There was a sweet story that read, "Grandma and I make cookies together." Another child told of playing checkers with Grandpa, and another of going to the zoo with Grandma and Grandpa.

As my eyes continued down the column, I moved a little chair and heard a squeal of delight from Aggie. "Here it is, Ma! You found it!" We squatted down together. I saw two extremely happy people in what looked like a car, smiling out the windshield. She told me that she had to use the name *Grandma* because the teacher helped her write the story. After studying the drawing, I read her account of our activity: "Grandma and I look for roadkill when we are out driving together."

I looked at the picture again. Sure enough, there was a carcass beside the car. I glanced at her as she stared at me, waiting for my response. I picked her up, swung her around, and told her it was the best story in the whole class. It certainly was the most original!

I must admit, this is something we actually do together. We were driving in the country one day, and I said, "Oh, look at the roadkill!"

"What's roadkill, Ma?"

"Dead animals along the side of the road."

"Oh, hey, let's go look for more!" And we did. We've continued "the hunt" for years. I never dreamed that looking for roadkill would be such a bonding experience for us. Now little Aggie can identify just about anything by the stub of a tail.

My granddaughter is out of elementary school now, and we don't look for roadkill quite as often as we used to, but I still love to get her in a car with me for a ride. It's one of the few times I have her full attention. She has learned some of my favorite worship songs and sings them with me, and we talk about her present and my past. I find any excuse to be with her and her bright little personality. So, whether it involves looking for roadkill, new clothes, or favorite snacks, one of my greatest joys is spending time with Aggie. It's a bonding thing!

Congenial conversation—what a pleasure!
The right word at the right time—beautiful!

PROVERBS 15:23 MSG

Jesus Loves the Little Children

— Gracie Malone —

Jesus loves me, this I know.
For the Bible tells me so.
Little ones to Him belong;
they are weak, but He is strong.

Anna B. Warner, from "Jesus Loves Me"

Watching our little ones growing up is the most blessed experience a grandmother can have. Especially when we see our grandkids beginning to comprehend spiritual truth, making decisions that honor God, and most importantly, believing in Him and then developing a meaningful relationship with the Lord. The aging apostle John spoke for grandmothers everywhere when he wrote, "I have no greater joy than this, to hear of my children walking in the truth" (3 John 4 NASB).

Such a walk begins when our offspring take a good, hard look at the truths they've been taught. After all, the parents' religion does not really belong to the child until he or she examines and accepts it. All three of our sons went through the painful process of feeling separated from God, asking questions, believing in his truth and grace, and taking a step of faith. The experience our son Mike had when he was eight is especially memorable to me.

One Sunday morning, Mike seemed disturbed by the preacher's message and spent the afternoon in deep thought. Then he came to me and said in an emotional tone, "Mom, I'm the only one in this family that's not a Christian."

After I answered a few of his questions, our little boy asked Jesus to come into his heart. The very next Sunday he was baptized. Joe and I rejoiced, not only because Mike had found peace but also in the fact that our family circle was now 100 percent Christian.

Of course, believing in Jesus was just the first step in our children's walk toward spiritual maturity. They learned to pray and, in their own unique ways, began to relate to God on an intimate level—first as their heavenly Father and eventually as their friend.

We've also seen this remarkable transformation take place in the lives of our grandchildren and other very young children. They not only become aware of God's presence at an early age but they also learn to trust him and are able to grasp deep spiritual truths. Their faith is able to see them through tough times, even some crises that would send some of us older folk into a spiritual nosedive.

Such strong faith was evident in a little girl named Jana. One day her grandma introduced her to me in a Christian bookstore. Then she relayed the following story.

It seems Jana was only five when she had to undergo serious open-heart surgery. The little girl was apprehensive, as any one of us would be under such circumstances. But in spite of her fear, Jana showed remarkable courage and strength. She believed in Jesus, and nothing could shake her faith.

Just before the frail girl went into the operating room, she looked up at her doctor and said, "I know you are going to open up my heart."

"That's right, sweetheart," the kindly doctor replied.

"Well," Jana thought for a few moments and then added, "when you open my heart, Jesus is in there. Don't take him out."

The doctor tenderly reassured the little girl, then turned toward the window to wipe away a stray tear and, perhaps, to breathe a prayer himself.

During the long, tedious procedure, Jesus stayed right there in Jana's fragile little heart—giving peace and comfort to the tiny sleeping patient. He was also present in the operating room, granting wisdom and skill to the medical team. Jana emerged from surgery with a healthy heart and has gone on to live many joyful, faith-filled years.

For I am convinced that neither death nor life,
neither angels nor demons, neither the present
nor the future, nor any powers, neither height
nor depth, nor anything else in all creation,
will be able to separate us from the love
of God that is in Christ Jesus our Lord.

ROMANS 8:38–39

Great Grandma's Autograph

— Jeanne Zornes —

More is caught than taught.

Unknown

We never had a heavy discussion about God and life, never even prayed together outside of mealtime grace. But she left her thumbprint on my life in a way I never expected.

I called her "Grandma Neely," though there should have been a "great" in front of that name. She was the only great grandmother I ever knew, and I knew little about her except what I noticed when she visited us and what I learned much later.

She devoted her last years to round-robin visits—a few weeks at this relative's home, then a few more weeks at another's. All welcomed her, this gentle widow whose native Norwegian tongue turned her second language, English, into gentle music.

I don't even recall who gave up a bed for Grandma Neely's visits, me or my sister. I only remember how she considered my dad's platform rocker, upholstered in well-worn red tapestry, her rightful place to sit. She'd stay there for hours, her worn black-leather Bible in her lap or resting on the lamp table and her crochet hook weaving thread. Sometimes the hook was motionless, and her eyes were closed. I never knew if she was napping or praying.

One day I decided I wanted her signature in my new red-covered autograph book. I'd gotten it for my tenth birthday and my friends had already signed its pastel pages.

Oh, the things little girls write:

"Two in a car, two little kisses, two weeks later, Mr. and Mrs."

"When you get old and think you're sweet, take off your shoes and smell your feet."

I knelt beside her and asked, "Can you sign my autograph book, Grandma Neely?" She put aside her knitting and smiled, her pale blue eyes sparkling behind her glasses. "I'll come back a little later," I promised. I wanted to give her enough time to recall a fantastic autograph ditty. With seventy-some years of life, she surely knew the best.

I'll never forget what she wrote. The meaning behind her carefully chosen autograph impacted me in a profound way. There, in her precise European script, was her name. And she had signed it under the sixteen words of 3 John 4: "I have no greater joy than to hear that my children are walking in the truth."

Years later, while working on our family history, I realized how her character had been forged in suffering and faith. She came to America as a small child. Her father died of a flu from the voyage. Her mother remarried another

Norwegian; then she died of tuberculosis. Her stepfather remarried, giving Grandma Neely double stepparents.

As an adult, Grandma Neely outlived two husbands. She opened her home to those in need, including a granddaughter who was the oldest of nine born to an impoverished Montana farmer and wife. She invited this young woman to come to Washington State and live with her and attend college—to get a better start in life. When that granddaughter married, Grandma Neely served as "mother of the bride." Now I understood the close relationship my mother—that granddaughter—had with her.

My memories of Grandma Neely were always connected to her well-used Bible. As a child, I wondered if I'd ever comprehend the Bible well enough to consider it my lifeline to God.

I got another glimpse of her faith just months before her death. My family was visiting her in a nursing home after her stroke. She struggled to communicate, but I understood this much: "I was on the Glory Road. I saw Jesus, but he wouldn't let me go on."

A few months later, she finished her journey on the Glory Road. But relatives never forgot her. One family member reported that for years Grandma Neely fasted and prayed once a week for her descendants. Dozens of people—including me—had their names and spiritual needs lifted to God in prayer.

Two decades later, my grandmother and my own parents

died within a couple years of one another. By then, I'd acutely sensed the torch of faith passed on to my generation, along with the need to pray for certain extended family members. Somehow, I wanted Grandma Neely to know her prayers for me were not in vain.

In the task of dissolving my parents' belongings, I came across my little autograph book, left at home in a pile of mementos. I opened its now-weathered red cover and smiled to read the silly ditties from friends. Then I turned with reverence to Great Grandma Neely's page.

Once again my eyes fell on Grandma's perfect European script, where she had signed her name, like a prophetic commission, under the verse I had read years earlier: "I have no greater joy than to hear that my children are walking in the truth."

Her quiet witness was still influencing my life.

Those who are wise will shine like the brightness of the heavens, and those who lead many to righteousness, like the stars for ever and ever.

DANIEL 12:3

Just Among Friends

– Gracie Malone –

Count your age by friends–not years;
count your life by smiles–not tears.

Unknown

My grandmother, Mama, was a dignified woman with roots that grew deep into the soil of Southern Baptist fundamentalism. This Christian woman would never, and I do mean never, say or do anything that could be considered crude or even a hair off-color. In fact, if a conversation took on even the slightest carnal innuendo, and she found it the least bit funny, Mama would cup her hand over her mouth so nobody could tell she was grinning. (At least she thought we couldn't tell!) Because she was so straitlaced, we were all surprised when we heard about an incident that happened in the nursing home where she lived out the last few years of her life.

Our Mama could almost always be found in the facility's living room with a circle of friends sitting around listening as she spun a tale or talked of days gone by. Every morning she'd climb into her wheelchair, propel herself down the hall—using a weird but highly effective combination of hand and foot movements—and edge her way into whatever conversation was taking place at the time. Sometimes she would join in a game of dominoes or help the other residents put together a puzzle. Mama would do almost anything to be in the mainstream of nursing home society.

While Mama loved being the life of the party, she tired easily, especially once she became ninety. But physical limitations were no problem for our feisty grandma. When she needed to rest, she could easily find her way back to her room. For as long as she had been in the nursing home, she'd lived on the east wing, third door on the left side of the hall, and occupied the bed on the right side of the room.

Unfortunately, after Mama had lived in the nursing home several years, we noticed that she was becoming more and more senile.

In the midst of this difficulty, the facility was refurbished, and Mama was moved to another room in the west wing. The east wing became the men's dormitory, and two gentlemen took up residence in Mama's old quarters. The move was more than a little disconcerting to my grandmother.

Nevertheless, she continued to make daily jaunts down the hall, into the living room, and somehow got back to her new location. But one morning on her way back to her room, she had a serious lapse of memory. In a troubling turn of events, she ended up in her old room, parked her wheelchair, and—climbed in bed with the man who now occupied her former space.

Apparently, the old fellow she warmed up to was of a sounder mind than our gregarious grandmother. For he told on Mama, suggesting to the nursing staff that my grandmother had acted in a, well, flirtatious manner.

This kind of news travels fast even in a place where everything else moves slowly. Before long, we found out all about Mama's misadventure. As the story goes, she snuggled up close to the gentleman, looked into his cloudy blue eyes, and spoke in a passionate tone, "Papa, at our age, I don't think we should have more than two kids."

As family members have passed this story down through the years since Mama's homegoing, some of us have snickered and blushed, and many of us have become angry at the nursing home staff who caused Mama's confusion in the first place. But whenever I hear the story retold, I can't help but smile. Mama lived long and brought us joy and laughter to the very end of her life. I hope I can do the same for my grandchildren.

> *A good life gets passed*
> *on to the grandchildren.*
>
> PROVERBS 13:22 MSG

The Blue Ford

— Laura Lee Leathers —

A pint of example is worth a barrelful of advice.

Unknown

Honk! Honk! The blue Ford blared as it approached our driveway. This was my grandmother's way of informing me I was late for Sunday school when I was not standing in my usual place, next to our gigantic silver mailbox.

"Bye, Mom," I yelled as I bolted out our front door. Rarely was Grandma early. Therefore, I felt justified waiting inside because there was no sense standing next to the dirt road until I knew she was coming. I also knew that I could be out the door and in her car before she came to a full stop. Once I was situated in the front seat, off she would go, taking on the winding, one-lane country dirt road as if she owned it.

The blue, eight-cylinder stick-shift Ford Fairlane was at her beck and call. She put it into first gear just long enough to take the first major curve to the right. With her foot on the clutch she shifted quickly into third gear, and off we would fly. Down the big hill, across the bridge, up and down another hill, and then she would slow down just enough to take a sharp curve to the left. It was a straight shot to the church after that. Only one stop sign could slow us down. Grandma would simply look to the left over the corn in the field, and if no cars were coming, she kept on going. Ahhh, I loved her sense of adventure.

A few minutes later Grandma parked the blue Ford by the side door of century-old LaMarsh Creek Baptist Church. It was my job to help Grandma get her stuff out of the car. Once I had her items properly placed on the desk, I would hurry to my class, where Mrs. Nowack was ready to teach the lesson. How I loved that woman! She could tell the best stories from the Bible.

After class it was back upstairs to the small sanctuary, where I sat next to Grandma for the church services. Little did I realize how much she was shaping my future. She showed me how to sing with gusto and how to place my offering in the plate. I watched her open the large, black-bound Bible, mark the date and the pastor's name next to the text he was reading, and then take notes on the back of an old envelope she pulled from her purse.

Week after week, year after year, my grandma and I repeated this procedure. My two younger sisters joined us when they reached the age of five. Looking back, I realize Grandma and her blue Ford not only took me to church but also to the ladies' quilting bee, ice cream socials, visits to church members, and to vacation Bible school. She was shaping my spiritual development. She taught me the importance of being at church and with God's people. Every place she took me was another opportunity for me to hear the Word of God and to connect with other Christians.

After Grandma died, her belongings were dispersed among relatives. I have to admit, I was a little disappointed when I received my box of items. It was all the leftovers no one else wanted. However, I now realize that God gave me exactly what I needed to remember—how Grandma had influenced my life. Among the items I received were several of her teacups, which have become a part of my collection. I use them in ministry. But the greatest treasure was her Bible. It even still had a few of her bookmarks and old envelopes inside.

Grandma and I spent many hours together over the years, and we had glorious adventures as we traveled in her blue Ford. But nothing compares to the adventures and the treasures I have discovered as I study my Bible each day. I'm thankful I had a grandma who demonstrated the importance of studying God's Word and being in church.

Recently I opened her Bible, and there on the left side of the aged white paper, she had written the following verse: "He that dwelleth in the secret place of the most High shall abide under the shadow of the Almighty ... He is my refuge and my fortress: my God; in him will I trust" (Psalm 91:1–2 KJV).

Grandma was still teaching me to trust in the absolute truth of God's Word.

Your word is a lamp for my feet,
a light on my path.

PSALM 119:105

911 Emergency

— Gracie Malone —

We plan, God laughs.

Old Yiddish proverb

When I located my phone and pushed the answer button, I quickly recognized the soft, ever-so-slightly trembling voice of my mom.

"Gracie, I think I broke my toe. I was getting something out of the freezer and when I let go of my walker, it fell forward and hit right on the big one. It's black-and-blue and swollen. I can't even wear my shoe. But you don't need to bother coming over. I've already doctored it with Campho-Phenique."

I couldn't help smiling as I hung up the phone. As far as my mother is concerned, camphorated oil can cure most anything, and what it can't fix, mentholated cream can. Her idea of a well-stocked medicine cabinet is a roll of cotton, a bottle of Campho-Phenique, Vicks salve, and a ChapStick. These have served her well for as long as I can remember, keeping her little body well-greased and operating efficiently for nearly a century. It's hard to argue with success.

I could tell that, even though she'd said not to come, Mom really needed a visit from the one she still calls her *baby girl*. Besides, I wanted to see for myself how serious her injuries were. I jumped in my car and headed to her house thirty minutes away.

Once there, I took off her sock and removed the oily ball of cotton to assess the damage. The toe was exactly as she'd described—bruised and swollen. But she could wiggle it, so I decided her home remedies would take care of the situation. I soaked the cotton with a fresh libation of oil and gently replaced her soft white sock. While she relaxed in her recliner and her foot nestled on a fluffy embroidered pillow, I warmed soup for her supper and vacuumed the living room. Then I kissed her goodbye and headed back home.

When I pulled into our driveway, I realized it was time for me to switch roles. I was no longer my mother's "baby girl." I was "Grandma Gracie" to the kids playing in our backyard. In a senior moment, I'd forgotten they were coming over to swim and roast hot dogs. As I parked and exited my car, the kids came a-running, throwing their wet little arms around me, slathering my cheeks with sloppy kisses.

Now I'll admit it takes a grandma to love it. But love it I do! Surrounded by all that affection, I felt a fresh burst of energy stirring deep within me. Like an Energizer Bunny with brand-new batteries, I whirled around and headed to start supper. Five-year-old Mary followed close behind.

"Grandma Gracie, can I have some chocolate milk?" she

began as she opened the pantry door and shuffled through the shelves looking for the Nestlé Quik. "Pleeeeeze, can I? Grandma Gracie, I'm dying!" I started to hand over the milk, thus not only saving the child's life but assuring my place as World's Nicest Grandma. But then I glanced out the window, eyed her parents, and decided to do the mature thing. Knowing they would not approve such a sugary concoction before dinner, I said no.

Mary begged. I felt compelled to stick with my answer.

The decision did not sit well with Mary. With her hands firmly planted on her hips, she huffed out of the kitchen, marched right into my bedroom, and called 911.

Imagine me trying to explain to the dispatcher, "There's no problem here. No, sir—except, well, I have my grandkids over here for supper and I wouldn't serve a chocolate milk appetizer."

As thy days, so shall thy strength be.

DEUTERONOMY 33:25 KJV

Sharing Grandchildren

— Linda Neff —

We make a living by what we get;
we make a life by what we give.

Unknown

The same year my mother turned eighty, she was scheduled for hip surgery. A few days later, I was allowed to take my four young children to the hospital for a brief visit. She was prepared.

After a long retirement following thirty years of teaching, the impulse to instruct never left her. When getting her things ready for the hospital stay, she had included a diagram of her surgical procedure. After our arrival, she produced it with enthusiasm from the bedside drawer. Carefully, she explained to her grandchildren what the surgeon had done.

Next, she dug into the same drawer and pulled out candy for the children. It had obviously been placed there in anticipation of their visit. Then my mother lifted the sheet from her leg and displayed her long bandage. Their eyes were wide with wonder. The bandage was so much larger than the ones that came out of the Band-Aid boxes for their small cuts and scrapes.

"Now," she whispered, "go to the next bed and say hello to Betty, my roommate. She doesn't get too many visitors. Remember, older people love the touch of young, unwrinkled skin, so be sure to take her hand."

I had never heard of someone sharing her hospital visitors with another patient. Betty, mother's roommate, was delighted with her enthusiastic young visitors.

How like my mother, I thought, to teach her grandchildren how to be compassionate in the middle of her own hospitalization. I quickly realized my mother was still teaching me, by example, how to demonstrate acts of kindness that make people feel valued, loved, and significant.

My children are almost grown now, and when I see them graciously reach out to others with compassion, I smile, knowing the gift of compassion has been passed to the next generation by a loving grandmother.

Dress in the wardrobe God picked out for you:
compassion, kindness, humility, quiet strength, discipline.
… And regardless of what else you put on, wear love.
It's your basic, all-purpose garment. Never be without it.

COLOSSIANS 3:12, 14 MSG

Long-Distance Grandmothers

— Gracie Malone —

If nothing is going well,
call your grandmother.

Italian proverb

What would we do without technology? It connects us to our grandchildren, some of whom live long distances from their doting grandparents. Even those who live close by seem to open up and talk more freely with some kind of electronic device cradled in their arms or pressed against their tiny ears.

As soon as my grandbabies learned to talk, they developed an affinity for the phone and, according to my daughters-in-law, would jump up and down excitedly whenever they got a call from their Grandma Gracie.

My grandson Connor seemed especially captivated by this manner of communication. When he was barely three, he would parade around the room with a phone in his hand mimicking the mannerisms of his dad, who could usually be found talking on his cell phone as he puttered around in the garage. At other times, Connor would sprawl on a chair, his tiny legs draped over the arm like a self-absorbed teen. I could hear him announce, as he cupped his hand over speaker, "It's for me. Please be quiet! It's Grandma Gracie."

Connor knew if he needed an extra dose of love and encouragement, he could usually count on his Grandma Gracie to come up with just the right words. *Usually!* One time when Connor called, I, being a bit preoccupied, didn't respond with my usual good cheer.

I was particularly busy when he phoned to relay some good news. "Grandma Gracie," he began, "I can swim … all the way across the pool."

"Really?"

"Yep … all the way across! Without my water wings."

My response time must have been a bit too slow, my tone a tad nonchalant, for I overheard his muffled voice as he cupped his hand over the speaker and muttered, "Dad, she didn't say, 'That's great!'"

Until that moment, I hadn't realized that I'd treated his good news in a less-than-enthusiastic manner. Nor did I realize how routinely I'd said those words— "That's great!" Feeling a bit chagrined, I quickly tried to correct my error. "Connor!" I yelled, "wait just a minute. Did you say you swam *all the way* across the pool? *Without* water wings? That's great, Connor! *Just great!*"

"Oh, thanks!" he answered. I know it isn't possible, but I actually thought I could *hear* his big grin as he handed the phone to his dad.

Unfortunately, this wasn't the only time I almost blew it with my young grandson.

One morning, my cell phone rang persistently. When I answered, I thought I recognized the voice of our older grandson, Luke. "Hey, Luke," I chirped.

"No!" the tiny voice on the other end of the line said in a perturbed tone. "It's me." Suddenly I realized my mistake, and like a kitten falling off the back of a chair, figured out a way to land on my feet.

"Of course it's you, Connor. It's just that, well—your voice sounded so grown-up. I guess I thought it was someone much older."

"Well, you've got that exactly right," Connor said confidently. Thankfully, Connor and I have managed to maintain a close relationship in spite of my verbal goofs.

It wasn't a week after the aforementioned mistake when he sauntered into the kitchen in his pajamas, handed his mom her phone and said, "Call Grandma Gracie. I have *sooo* many things I want to say to her."

I'm glad Connor knows that in spite of my blunders, I really care about the details of his everyday life.

*Gently encourage the stragglers, and reach out
for the exhausted, pulling them to their feet.
Be patient, … attentive to individual needs.…
Be cheerful no matter what, … This is the way
God wants you who belong to Christ Jesus to live.*

1 THESSALONIANS 5:14, 16–18 MSG

Caught on Film!

— Ginger Kamps —

Prayer is not overcoming God's reluctance;
it is laying hold of His highest willingness.

Richard Chenevix Trench

My daughter Traci called me on the phone, her voice trembling. She was crying. "Mom!" she blurted out between sobs. "The test was negative. I am not pregnant!"

Traci and Kevin had been married two years, and they had been trying to conceive for several months to no avail. Traci was sure this time was it, but the in-home pregnancy test told her otherwise.

What a disappointment! My heart broke for my daughter, and I struggled to find words to console her. "Oh, I am so sorry, honey. Don't be upset. It will happen in God's perfect timing." I tried to be optimistic and upbeat.

"But I was sure I was pregnant this time, and now the test says I'm not," Traci cried. "I want to have a baby!" Her heartfelt sobs broke my heart, and I cried with her.

"Well, honey," I said bravely, "keep praying. We will just have to trust God for positive results next time."

We hung up the phone, and I went to my prayer room, our home library. Lined with bookshelves on three walls, it smells of leather and wood. Beneath the window sits an old oak library table, and standing next to it is a solid oak chair where I've placed a genuine, made-in-Israel, Jewish prayer shawl. I had given it to my mother as a gift, and when she passed away, it came back to me. The oak chair became my altar that day as I knelt in prayer to seek God on behalf of my barren daughter.

As I called out to God, tears rolled down my cheeks. Traci was my firstborn. I had miscarried my second child, and my son, Perry, was my third. I'd become a mother at a young age and had no trouble conceiving, so I hadn't experienced my daughter's pain.

That day a scripture I had memorized came back to me: "We do not know what we ought to pray for, but the Spirit himself intercedes for us through wordless groans" (Romans 8:26). I struggled for the words to pray for my daughter. As I agonized in my communication with God that day, my words, emotions, and fervent cries were sent heavenward as I pleaded with him to grant my daughter's request for a child.

Two weeks later, Traci called again. "Mom," she said with a lilt in her voice, "I went to the pregnancy center and had a pregnancy test. I'm pregnant!"

Several weeks later Traci had her first ultrasound, and she joyously brought the pictures over to show me and my husband, Kenny. I had become ill very suddenly that day and was sleeping when she brought the picture into the bedroom. I could barely raise my head, and between half-closed eyes, I groggily looked at the little piece of black-and-white paper she clutched. I was trying hard to see the outline of a baby in the picture, but it just wasn't registering.

Traci said, "Look closer, Mom. Do you see it?"

I looked again and saw an arrow and a letter of the alphabet next to dark and light shadows. Now it was becoming clearer. There were two letters of the alphabet with arrows, an A and a B.

Traci once again said, "Do you see it?" her voice growing with impatience.

There they were—not one baby, but *two* babies in her womb! I sat straight up in my bed, finally understanding that my first grandbaby would actually be two! Joy flooded the room!

We thought back on the timeline and realized that when Traci called with the negative result of the first pregnancy test, she was, in fact, very early in her pregnancy. We believe that my fervent prayer for her that day may have caused the egg to split and become two identical, little twin girls. Every day I thank God for allowing me to be "Grandma Ginger" to the beautiful grandchildren he brought into my life. Those precious babies, once "caught on film" in their mother's womb, are my crowning joy!

Children's children are a crown to the aged.

PROVERBS 17:6

All Creatures Small
– Gracie Malone –

All creatures great and small ...
The Lord God made them all.

Cecil Alexander, from "All Things Bright and Beautiful"

My sister Lois's three-year-old great grandson, Ashton, is what we older folks refer to as "all boy." That means he loves dirt, sticks, rocks, and anything else that relates to the great outdoors—including four-footed creatures and bugs. One afternoon, Lois called to tell me the following story.

***

Ashton came running into his grandma's house with a big smile on his face and his little hand clenched into a tiny fist. "Grandma, guess what I've got in my hand!" He extended his arm in Lois's direction. He unfolded his fingers and proudly showed off his latest discovery—a tiny, gray, multi-jointed creature known in Texas as a "roly-poly" bug. The little bug had rolled itself into a tiny ball no bigger than a BB with its hairy legs tucked inside.

As Ashton held it forward on his palm, the little creature suddenly fell to the floor, where it unrolled and started crawling across the carpet. Ashton got down on his hands and knees, crawled alongside it for a while, and then watched the little bug creep toward his grandma's chair. After a few minutes, he picked it up, brought his hand close to his mouth and spoke tenderly, "Where are you going, little roly-poly?" With eyes shining, he turned toward his grandma. Since she didn't appear squeamish at all, he dropped the tiny bug into her palm.

As Lois sat there cradling the tiny creature, her mind flooded with memories, including days when she was a little girl with little else to play with than the creatures in her backyard. "When I was growing up, I played with roly-poly bugs too," she explained. Then she told Ashton about coaxing doodlebugs out of their cone-shaped home in the sand, putting lightning bugs in a jar where she could watch their fluorescent glow cast an eerie light through the glass container. She remembered tying a string around the middle of an old locust and hearing its loud humming as it flew in circles overhead like a tiny, tethered airplane. Lois paused before adding, "I played with ladybugs too."

That sparked something in Ashton's little mind. "Poppie and G. G. have ladybugs in their backyard!" Lois remembered when her son and daughter-in-law, with Ashton's help, created a flowerbed for Texas wildflowers. They purchased a large quantity of ladybugs from a garden catalog to release in that bed to help control harmful insects. Ashton loved to watch the ladybugs spread their red, dotted wings and fly from one bloom to another.

Later that evening, Lois took another jaunt down memory lane, stopping to recall the days when one of her own little boys—Jerry, Tommy, or Larry—would run in the house after playing outside in their big backyard. She recalled the musty smell of dirt and sweat, the salty kisses on their foreheads, the dirty fingernails from digging in the sandbox, that ring of dust we called "grandma's beads" caught in the wrinkles of their neck, and little roly-poly bugs clenched in their fists.

"You know, Ashton," Lois said, "even though years come and go and generations multiply, some things never change. And sometimes it's the little things in life that bring us the greatest joy."

I look up at your macro-skies, dark and enormous,
  your handmade sky-jewelry,
 Moon and stars mounted in their settings.
 Then I look at my micro-self and wonder,
  Why do you bother with us? ...
Yet ... You put us in charge of your handcrafted world,
  repeated to us your Genesis-charge,
 Made us stewards of sheep and cattle,
  even animals out in the wild,
 Birds flying and fish swimming,
  whales singing in the ocean deeps.
  God, brilliant Lord,
 your name echoes around the world.

PSALM 8:3–9 MSG

Grandma is Online

— Bonnie Afman Emmorey —

*The real trick is to stay
alive as long as you live.*

Ann Landers

They had little in common, but they connected. It started several years ago. My son Jordan was in his early teens. Grandma was in her early seventies. Jordan was one of the finest cross-country runners in the state of Michigan. Grandma did water aerobics with "old people." Jordan loved fast food and soda. Grandma made the equivalent of a Thanksgiving dinner on a daily basis. Jordan loved cappuccino and lattes. Grandma drank one cup of decaf a day. Jordan made straight A's in school. Grandma made puzzles.

When the Internet became available to the masses, my mother thought she was too old to learn anything new, yet she took to it like a teenager. Jordan *was* a teenager. Over the next few years, new topics of conversation emerged. From fonts to servers and everything in between, Jordan and Grandma connected. When Grandma had a fatal error appear on her screen, Jordan was her first call. Jordan said,

"Grandma, you need to take a basic computer class. You would learn so much and feel more confident."

Grandma was not excited. "I'm too old. My brain can't possibly take in and remember anything so technical."

"Wait just a minute, Grandma. Your brain is just like a computer that has had so much information put into it that it feels like it might crash. Don't worry! It won't! It just needs to be organized and filed properly, and it might take you a bit longer to pull up certain information, but you definitely still have access to everything. You're a top-of-the-line model! But remember, when I leave for college, I won't be as available to fix your computer glitches."

Jordan was confident that Grandma, even at her advanced age, would benefit from going back to school. And she did. He made many six-hour round trips to Grandma's house to work with her and her computer. She became gifted at creating unique and special greeting cards made especially for each recipient. Grandma adapted to new technology, and she communicated daily with friends and family via email.

When she upgraded to a new computer, Jordan rejoiced with her. One Christmas, Jordan and his brother bought Grandma the best printer they could find, one better than either of them had themselves. They were more excited about giving that one gift and watching her open it than about opening their own presents.

As I watched that scene, thinking of all the time Jordan spent with Grandma and how important she had become to him, my heart rejoiced. I had always been jealous of my friends who had their parents living in the same town with them, ready to babysit and spend time with their grandchildren. Who would have guessed that my son would develop such a close relationship with a grandmother who lived hours away?

When Jordan left for Columbia University in New York City, I was amazed when he made spending time with Grandma a priority during his brief visits home. She still called him when she had a computer glitch, and he continued to help her fix minor problems. Grandma had Jordan's cell number on speed dial, and in time, she purchased her own smartphone. Who would have thought they would have so much in common?

Look for the best in each other,
and always do your best to bring it out.

I THESSALONIANS 5:15 MSG

Friends with God

— Gracie Malone —

Dear God, I think about you sometimes,
even when I'm not praying.
Love, Elliott

Unknown

I love the sincere, no-nonsense prayers of children. Even though most of them have never taken a course on how to pray or memorized a single prayer promise from the Bible, they can teach us older folk a thing or two about talking to God.

For one thing, children have no problem being thorough in their prayers. They are quite comfortable sharing every detail with our heavenly Father, especially when they're expressing thanks. When our son Matt was a kid and he took his turn offering the blessing at mealtimes, the dialog usually went something like this: "Thank you, God, for the mashed potatoes, and gravy, and, *mmm*, the corn, and the bread and butter. And most of all for the dessert. (What's for dessert, Mom? Chocolate pudding?) Thanks for the chocolate pudding! Amen."

I've also noticed that children are not timid when it comes to asking for God's blessing. When it came time for bedtime prayers, our preschool son, Mike, would mention everybody in our family, our circle of friends, and all sorts of spiritual and national leaders. Matt was usually the one to put the caboose on Mike's endless train of "God blesses" by jumping in with a hearty and heartfelt "Amen."

And I'm not the only matriarch who's been pleasantly surprised at the way her offspring present their requests in prayer. They have no problem identifying their needs and asking God to meet them. My friend Anita told me how her granddaughter, Katie, taught her to be specific in her prayers. Katie is a sensitive little girl with special needs. She loves babies, but simply cannot endure their crying.

One day when Anita was babysitting her four-month-old grandson, Cade, the baby was especially cranky. As the evening progressed, he burst into tears several times. Every time he cried, Katie got wound up too. "Please make him stop," Katie whimpered. "Why is Cade so unhappy?"

Anita had her hands full. She would bounce the baby, then wipe Katie's tears, bounce the baby, and wipe Katie's tears. Finally, Cade quieted down and Anita pulled Katie onto her lap. "Cade isn't sad or unhappy, sweetheart," she patiently explained, "he cries because he feels uncomfortable, wants a bottle, or needs his diaper changed. You know, babies can't talk, so when they need something they just cry."

Katie seemed to understand, but she still didn't like it.

When the baby finally went to sleep and Katie was ready for bed, the little girl knelt to say her prayers. "Dear Lord," she began fervently, "puh-leeeze help Cade learn to talk!"

Perhaps the most important aspect of prayer is simply recognizing God's presence and relating to him with spontaneity and freedom. It's a concept our little grandson Luke was able to grasp at an early age.

Luke and his little brother, Connor, were visiting with me while their mom and dad took a weekend trip. Early one morning, the boys stumbled into the living room and climbed in my lap for a hug. As we rocked back and forth in my chair, rays of bright sunshine filtered through the open shutters, bounced off the prism hanging in my kitchen window, and cast rainbows of brilliant color on the white walls. When Luke spotted the rainbows, he rubbed his eyes, slipped out of my chair, and stood transfixed for a moment. Then with a flash of insight and in a tone of reverence and awe, he announced, "Grandma Gracie, God is here!"

Connor wiggled out of my lap, and both little boys began jumping up and down in the sparkling light, making a myriad of colors dance across their faces. As they laughed and danced in the bright sunshine, I felt God's presence too.

Not long after this spiritual experience, Luke decided he'd tired of saying a memorized prayer. He was ready to talk to God in his own words. One night he and his daddy (the aforementioned Matt) talked about it. "God is your friend, Luke," Matt began. "You can say anything you want to him."

Luke quickly understood the concept. Later that evening when they knelt together beside the bed, Luke talked freely, like a child talking to a good friend that he trusted and loved. Then he concluded his prayer with, "Goodbye, Jesus; have a nice day."

"I have called you friends,
for everything that I learned
from my Father I have
made known to you."

JOHN 15:15

Who's the Boss?

— Carol Kent —

*Life is no "brief candle" to me.
It is sort of a splendid torch,
which I have got hold of for a moment,
and I want to make it burn as
brightly as possible before handing
it on to future generations.*

George Bernard Shaw

We were nearing the end of Thanksgiving weekend, and my husband and I were visiting our son and his family in Florida. After preparing multiple meals of leftover turkey and mashed potatoes, all of us were ready for a change of menu. Hannah, age eight, volunteered to go with me on a run to Taco Bell.

Ah, I thought. This time alone with Hannah will give me an opportunity to let her know how precious she is to me, and I might get a chance to find out where she's coming from spiritually at this time in her life.

Waiting at a red light, I queried, "Hannah, have you thought about what you want to be when you grow up?"

"Yes," she quickly responded. "I want to be a movie star so I can make a million bucks!"

"What would you do with that much money?" I asked.

She needed no extra time for thoughtful consideration of how to spend her fortune. "I'd buy me a Hummer!"

The speed of her response surprised me, so I immediately asked, "What would you do with a vehicle that big?"

Without pausing for air, she said, "Oh, Grammy, I'd pick up all of the lost and hurt dogs and take care of them."

I was struck by her obvious compassion and with the thought she had put into her response. This was a subject she had considered long before I asked the question. Still, I wanted to go deeper and discover what she was thinking about her destiny and about her relationship with the Lord. "Hannah, what do you think you would like to do for God when you grow up?"

Crossing her arms with a bit of defiance, she looked at me with conviction and stated emphatically: "I think I would like to *be* him, because then I could be the boss of me!"

I didn't have an immediate comeback because her reply took me by surprise. Before long she was singing out loud in the passenger seat and within minutes we were ordering our take-out dinner. We soon returned home with our arms filled with tacos, burritos, and nachos, and we enjoyed a lively family meal together.

Later I thought about Hannah's namesake in the Bible— a woman with a strong desire for a son, who believed God would grant her request. Hannah prayed. God answered. And the course of history was changed. I wondered how my strong-willed Hannah would change the course of history. My thoughts turned into a prayer as I pondered that important conversation with my granddaughter:

> Lord, thank you for placing Hannah in my life. Her personality is enthusiastic, vibrant, and alive. She makes me laugh out loud at unexpected moments. Her will is strong, and her responses are not always what I expect. I know you have a powerful work to do in her heart. Help me to be sensitive to her questions and wise with my responses. Lord, I pray that you will mold her will to yours and that she will soon discover the greatest joy comes in letting you be in charge of her life.

That holiday weekend visit has been a constant reminder of the importance of praying for my granddaughters. I think it's the most important job I have!

I desire to do your will, my God;
your law is within my heart.

PSALM 40:8

Fit for a Queen

— Gracie Malone —

Brain cells come and brain cells go,
but fat cells live forever.

Unknown

As the story goes, a rather large woman was lumbering down the aisle in the grocery store picking up items along the way. Her preschool grandson was tagging along, asking questions about every item she selected.

Let me preface this part of the story by explaining that in the late sixties the L'eggs brand of pantyhose radically changed the hosiery marketplace with their egg-shaped plastic product container.

The woman paused at one of those "Legg's Eggs" pantyhose displays, made her choice, and tossed the package into the cart. The shape of the package must have piqued the youngster's curiosity, for the little guy almost tipped the cart over as he climbed over and retrieved the package from the bottom of the basket. He clutched the item in his tiny extended hand and in a booming tone sounded out the words on the label: "Queen size!"

As several nearby shoppers turned to look, the red-faced grandma grabbed the item from the child's hand, but not before he shouted, "Grandma, are these the same size as our mattress?"

When I heard this tale, I couldn't hold back a snarky giggle. That poor grandma must have been soooo embarrassed! But I giggled for another reason as well. For I can identify with this young man's confusion. How can something "queen-sized" be squeezed into a package no bigger than an egg? Furthermore, why is it when a pair of "queen-size" hose is removed from the package and unfurled, it seems more "fit" for Tinker Bell than a queen?

As I thought about this story, I remembered facing my own battle with a pair of pantyhose one Sunday morning as I was getting ready for church. I had carefully opened a package of so-called queen-size hosiery and shook out the wrinkles. As I examined the eight-inch waistband trying to locate the back, the tiny undergarment's twelve-inch-long legs floated on the air like a pair of butterfly wings. I couldn't help but wonder about the elasticity of the nylon fibers as I held the garment up to the light. It was then that I noticed my hubby watching me. He took one look at the minuscule pair of pantyhose, patted me on my, well, rather *ample* backside, and with great conviction in his voice proclaimed, "I believe in miracles!"

Sure enough, I was able to pull on those pantyhose and still manage to walk. In fact, I not only wore them to church but also to the drugstore the next day when I went shopping with my six-year-old granddaughter, Mary Catherine.

The little girl stood close beside me as I examined a line of cosmetics, trying to find just the right moisturizer. (Decisions, decisions!) Mary, truly a girly-girl who loves to play with makeup, seemed caught up in the process. After a few minutes she selected a well-advertised brand of cream, and in a loud tone suggested, "Grandma Gracie, here! Try this Oil of Ole Lady."

Sometimes I think God gives us grandchildren to keep us humble. For we can always count on them to give an opinion based upon the unabashed, unadulterated truth. But even though they see us just as we are, our precious grandkids really don't care if we're fat or thin, tall or short, drop-dead gorgeous, or wrinkled and gray. They love us unconditionally with the most amazing selfless love we'll ever experience this side of heaven.

Is there a grandma among us who couldn't use a liberal dose of that kind of devotion? Seems to me that's love fit for a queen.

If we love one another,
God dwells deeply within us,
and his love becomes
complete in us—perfect love!

I JOHN 4:12 MSG

Joy Cakes and Magic Teeth

— Annetta Dellinger —

Inject a spirit of joy and optimism into your
grandchildren. Do it by example! Begin now!

Unknown

I *loved* Easter weekend! It wasn't the lure of a new dress
or the old apple orchard with honeysuckle vines where I
played hide-and-seek in the branches, or the lush spring
grass that hid rainbow-colored eggs that got me the most
excited about my annual trip to Grandma's house. It was
the opportunity of helping to bake a lamb-shaped cake that
always kept me asking, "How many days until Easter?"

It was amazing how making the "Joy Cakes," as Grandma
called them, would somehow take all day. She told stories
about our family roots while she did silly things like remov-
ing and repositioning her magical teeth. We'd laugh until
our sides hurt. Secretly I'd wait for her to dust flour on my
face and take lots of pictures. Even though she told me that
looking that way would make the cake taste better, I knew
it was really so she could say to her friends, "Look at my
granddaughter!"

While I helped her mix up icing (of which there was always enough extra to lick the spoons), we sang "I Am Jesus' Little Lamb" and talked about the Good Shepherd's constant protection and everlasting love. Before I realized it, we had once again recited Psalm 23. Learning with her was such fun. I can still see the twinkle in her eye when she would say, "Ewe is loved by Jesus and me!"

When Grandma went to live with the Good Shepherd, my mother joyfully inherited her cake pans. She laughed and lovingly told me she would carry on the tradition when she had grandchildren. And she certainly did! Hearing my children talk about their day at Grandma's house (and her magic teeth) made my heart burst with joy. I was already dreaming of the day when hopefully I, too, would have such a physical and spiritual influence as a grandmother—but without the false teeth.

Now I am once again counting days, along with my grandchildren, until the ewes come for the bake-off. We laugh, lick, and learn—plus we've added two new traditions. First, while we are busy in the kitchen creating memories, we discuss who we should surprise with one of the cakes. We think about church members who are shut-ins, families with little children, Sunday school teachers, and neighbors, with the list getting longer each year. After the decision is made and the cake is finished, the children carefully carry it to the car and hold it steady as I drive around the curves. The children try to control their nervous laughter while thinking about how surprised our recipient will be. When the lamb cake is transferred to the unsuspecting person, the joyful faces of the givers are as animated as that of the receiver.

The second tradition I've added is to talk about the reason we have Easter and God's gift of salvation. I ask my grandchildren, "If you died right now, would 'ewe' go to heaven? Why?" In fact, the grandkids now see if they can ask *me* before I challenge them! It's a joy to know we will all be together with the Good Shepherd someday.

The older I get, the more I realize that my grandmother had a method to her madness, and now I'm a copycat. She took the time to prove her belief that whatever is written on the heart of a child, good or bad, will never be washed away with time. I, too, believe that each of us leaves a legacy. I caught my grandmother's love for Jesus, and I pray I'm contagious with that joy too. It's the reason she called the lamb-shaped cakes Joy Cakes.

For we are God's handiwork,
created in Christ Jesus to do
good works, which God prepared
in advance for us to do.

EPHESIANS 2:10

In the Eye of the Beholder

— Gracie Malone —

Let me grow lovely, growing old–
so many fine things do:
Laces, and ivory, and gold,
and silks need not be new;
And there is healing in old trees,
Old streets a glamour hold;
Why may not I, as well as these,
Grow lovely, growing old?

Karle Wilson Baker, "Let Me Grow Lovely"

My mother must have been in her late eighties when she had her picture taken for her church's pictorial directory. She had selected a lovely dress and, in my humble but biased opinion, looked absolutely *mahvelous* for a gal of her age. She, on the other hand, seemed a bit disappointed with her likeness. "I guess it looks okay," she began, "but, well … my neck looks like an old turkey."

Not being one to hold back an opinion, I took one look at her sagging skin and quipped, "Mom, for an eighty-something-year-old neck, I think it looks fabulous." Then

I tickled her under the chin and went, "Gobble, gobble." At that, Mother giggled happily. But just a few years later, a similar situation occurred.

On her ninetieth birthday we celebrated on a grand scale. Her children, grandchildren, great grandchildren, and a few great-greats gathered at First Baptist Church where she'd been a member for more than sixty years. The mayor came and issued a proclamation honoring my mom as "Most Worthy Citizen" of Farmers Branch.

We took pictures—gobs of pictures—which she loved and still peruses to this day. She loved them all, except maybe for one. It was a warm photo that I was especially proud of because it depicted four generations from my branch of the family tree—Mom, me, my daughter-in-law Jeanna, and baby Myles, just two months old. I couldn't keep from flashing the photo to anybody who would sit still long enough to take a look. Until, that is, one day when my mom put her hand on my shoulder and whispered, "I don't like that picture. Just look at my hands." Only then did I notice the gnarled knuckles and bulging purple veins.

Looking at those hands that through the years of my life had diapered me, washed my face, wiped away tears, packed my lunch, handed over car keys, tucked an antique hanky in my pocket on the day of my wedding, and were now holding my precious grandbaby, I couldn't stop the lump rising in my throat. I choked out the words, "Those hands are beautiful to me." Mother smiled sweetly.

Later, I wondered, *When will we women give up the idea that beauty means being perfectly groomed, rail thin, and wrinkle-free?* My guess is, until eternity, when we will be sporting a brand-new, perfect body!

Meanwhile, as we live out our lives here on planet Earth, we need to encourage each other to take a deeper look at what's really important, to put aside our longings to present a perfect outward image and focus on things of eternal value. We could follow the example of a young deacon from my mother's church.

One Sunday morning, after a hymn, the worship leader invited the members of the congregation to greet one another. When my mom turned around and took the deacon's hand, he looked directly into her big brown eyes, saw past the crow's feet that crinkled at the corners, and got a glimpse into her soul. He uttered one word: "Beautiful!"

It's absolutely amazing what one word can do!

Even today, years after the tiny compliment was uttered, my mom loves to remind us of what that deacon said. If I could find that man today, I'd like to tell him his compliment was, well—absolutely *beautiful*!

And we all, who with unveiled faces
contemplate the Lord's glory,
are being transformed into his
image with ever-increasing glory,
which comes from the Lord,
who is the Spirit.

2 CORINTHIANS 3:18

The White Tornado

— Bobbie Rill —

*The foolish man seeks happiness in the
distance; the wise grows it under his feet.*

James Oppenheim

My husband and I have been empty nesters for several years. But before the revolving door came to a complete stop, we realized our two children were actually going to make it. They had developed into fully functioning adults who would soon be on their own.

A strange thing happened. I began noticing a quirky smile forming on my lips, and occasionally I noticed Bob suppressing the same grin. It was as though we both knew it wouldn't be long before the house would be solely ours! But shouldn't we feel sad? Was it really okay to be happy—perhaps even to celebrate? Taking the advice of friends, we headed for our favorite home-furnishings showroom with a gleam in our eyes and a spring in our step.

We had visited the store numerous times before, but this visit was different. This time we were serious shoppers. We were ready to redecorate the house from top to bottom and to replace the worn-out furniture. Entering the store, we both enthusiastically went our separate ways. Bob found a beautiful leather sofa. My head pivoted from kitchen tables to new furniture for the patio, to glass tables, which would serve beautifully as accent pieces throughout our new home. We left feeling good that day—without any sense of buyers' remorse.

Then Skyler Ashton Elder, affectionately known to us as the White Tornado, entered our lives! At fourteen months, with his curly blond hair and sparkling blue eyes, Skyler literally hit the floor running when our daughter, Brigette, put him down.

Since ours is not a childproofed house, I followed close behind. Skyler ran into the family room as though he had mapped out his destination before his arrival. Swinging his arms, he weaved around the island that separates the family room from the kitchen, headed toward a protruding chair, then went directly to the table by the telephone.

After he cleared the table of some toys that I had strategically placed near the edge (thinking I would be way ahead of him), Skyler stretched, lifting up on one leg, and claimed a yellow highlighter near the back of the table as his special "find." While snapping the lid off and on, he moved to his next stop, the coffee table, where several *Better Homes & Gardens* and *Gourmet* magazines were displayed. He thumbed through the one on top before I was able to rescue the stack.

Next he was drawn to a plant. He stuck his little fingers into the soil and came up with a handful of dirt and pebbles. I was barely able to throw the stack of magazines down in time to stop the pebbles from entering his mouth. I brushed off his hand and headed for a cloth in the kitchen, but before I returned, Skyler had located his supply of toys stored near the entertainment center.

With books and toys now strewn all over the family room, Skyler backed up to the fireplace hearth, placed one elbow on the ledge, leaned back, and paused briefly, wondering who this crazy lady was heading toward him with a damp cloth to wash his hands and face. Sponged clean, he was off again. He had been in the house less than two minutes and already I was exhausted. Obviously, "keeping up with Skyler" was a useless endeavor, and I plopped down on the sofa.

When Skyler and his mother left that afternoon, I immediately went for the Windex, grabbed the paper towels, and headed for the coffee table. I was just about to remove the evidence of Skyler's presence when I was stopped cold in my tracks. There, on my glass table, was the complete imprint of his hands. I stepped back, staring at his handprints all over the glass table, and I couldn't bring myself to erase the impressions of my grandson's presence.

I'm discovering how to clear the path better—*before* Skyler's visits. But more importantly, I'm learning how to take pleasure in our time together, and I enjoy the evidence of his visits after he leaves. The door of my heart and my home will always be open to that child. And I wouldn't trade those tiny fingerprints all over my house for anything in the world!

My little "white tornado" reminds me that even when I mess things up, my heavenly Father loves me and enjoys my presence.

> *"I have loved you with an everlasting love;*
> *I have drawn you with unfailing kindness."*
>
> JEREMIAH 31:3

The Sponge Factor

— Bonnie Afman Emmorey —

Children are sponges—they are going to absorb whatever is around them, so we need to be intentional about what surrounds them.

Dave Ramsey

It seems like yesterday that my own sons were young, and now they are fathers and I'm an Oma (Dutch for grandma). As I watch my grands, I see sponges. They seem to soak up everything. E.V.E.R.Y.T.H.I.N.G. All the good, the bad, and the ugly.

Fortunately, our sons are excellent fathers, and they married women who are amazing mothers. This was evident when our three-year-old grandson came for a visit. We lived in a big, old house filled with fun spaces. One spot next to the stairway to the basement was a particular enticement. On a ledge was a large old cabinet, and on top of it was a row of antique candy jars filled with old-style penny candy. Because of its location at the top of the stairway, only a tall person could reach the candy. However, there was an antique hall tree connected to a bench on the landing.

The adults were in the kitchen with a full view to this tempting area watching my grandson Nash, who had decided he could reach the candy jars if he climbed on the seat of the hall tree and reached as far as he could. It might have been the laughter coming from the kitchen that alerted him that he was being observed, but he turned with indignation and said, "Stop watching me. I'm making poor choices!"

Obviously more laughter followed, but I was impressed with two things. First, at three years of age, Nash already knew the difference between good choices and poor choices, and secondly, his parents had been the ones to teach him that very important lesson.

One day my husband, Ron, and I were watching Nash and his three younger sisters while their parents were away. Again I was impressed with the fact that they notice *everything*, and they constantly ask questions.

Early Sunday morning I was cuddling with the three girls on my lap and four-year-old Nell looked up at me intently. She studied my face. With a surprised look, she asked, "Oma, what happened to your eyebrows?"

With a bit of groan followed by my own laughter, I said, "Nell, they sort of disappeared over time." She seemed satisfied with my answer.

Before long it was time to get ready for church, and I went into the bathroom to put on my makeup and get dressed. Two little girls followed asking if they could watch. Before long I was adding some color to my eyebrows, and they looked at me in amazement. "You do it like that?" I had to admit it was true. I privately hoped I was not teaching them to add extra eyebrows to their own beautiful little faces.

On the journey home from church, we talked through all they had learned in Sunday school and sang some of their favorite songs. Suddenly, from the third row of the vehicle, I heard the voice of three-year-old Tess call out, "I want eyebrows!"

I'm learning that they are all sponges, and I better guard my words and actions. They *will* be copied. Let's hope all the Sharpies are under lock and key.

> Train up a child in the way he should go;
> even when he is old he will not depart from it.

PROVERBS 22:6 ESV

Coming of Age

— Gracie Malone —

*Family faces are magic mirrors.
Looking at people who belong to us,
we see the past, present, and future.*

Gail Lumet Buckley

Now that they are widows living alone, my eighty-four-year-old mother and her slightly younger sisters, my Aunt Grace and Aunt Oreta, enjoy spending an occasional weekend together. My older sister, Lois, always comes along as Mother's chauffeur, and I usually join them just in case somebody falls and can't get up. These weekends are fun for all of us—three lazy days replete with stories about our kinfolk and chock-full of Texas comfort food, including fried chicken, homemade pies, and sweet iced tea.

One evening, according to our usual after-dinner routine, we gathered in the living room, kicked back in five recliners, and started a conversation typical of a bunch of "Golden Girls." We began by discussing the peculiar problems of those who are, well, "chronologically gifted."

Mother said that as a person ages, her nose grows longer

and her ears get bigger. I had to admit it was an anomaly I'd never even noticed! I also wondered if I would notice now every time I passed a mirror. I shook my head and contributed to the conversation by suggesting that such a development must be God's warning signal that the basic five senses will need some extra help in the declining years. This touched off a barrage of silly conclusions. We had all noticed how older folks get hard of hearing, but, we wondered, do they also get "hard of smelling"?

From there, the conversation moved on to the subject of hair, and we concluded that most members of the older generation lose hair up top and it sprouts in the most bizarre places. Which brings me to what has become the infamous story of my mother's aversion to such stray hairs.

One bright Saturday morning during one of the aforementioned weekend visits, we decided to go see my one-hundred-and-three-year-old grandmother, Mama, who lived in a nursing home. I settled into the backseat of the car next to my mom as Lois and Oreta climbed up front with Aunt Grace. Bright sunshine gleamed through the rear window as we rode along. Feeling good about being the youngest member of the group, I closed my eyes, content to listen to the older women's chitchat. I opened my eyes when I heard my mom fumbling through her purse.

From the depths of her bag, Mother retrieved a shiny steel instrument and began polishing it with her hanky. I wondered what she was doing until I recognized her tweezers. Without one word of warning, my mother took aim and plucked my chin. Then she proudly displayed her prize: one curly, half-inch-long silver hair. Her mission accomplished, she replaced the tweezers in their leather case and deposited them back in her purse without missing a beat in the conversation.

As I rubbed my chin, I felt a bit perturbed at my mom for the not-so-subtle reminder that I'm aging, myself. To be honest, I was not quite ready to accept senior citizen status. I felt better a few days later when I turned to the book of Psalms and read about God's faithfulness. "The LORD is trustworthy in all he promises and faithful in all he does. The LORD upholds all who fall and lifts up all who are bowed down. The eyes of all look to you, and you give them their food at the proper time. You open your hand and satisfy the desires of every living thing" (Psalm 145:13–16).

That evening, when I rested my graying head on my pillow, my fear of growing older seemed to vanish. I whispered a prayer, thanking God for three generations of women who have walked through life ahead of me, loved me well, and, in their own unique way, prepared me to face the future with confidence. What more could a woman need? Except, well, maybe tweezers—and a well-lighted magnifying mirror.

"*Even to your old age and gray hairs
I am he, I am he who will sustain you.
I have made you and I will carry you;
I will sustain you and I will rescue you.*"

ISAIAH 46:4

About Carol Kent, General Editor

Carol Kent is a best-selling author and international speaker. With vulnerable openness, irrepressible hope, restored joy, and a sense of humor, she directs you to choices based on God's truth. Carol says, "When God writes your story, you will be in for the adventure of a lifetime!"

Carol is the executive director of the Speak Up Conference, a ministry committed to helping Christians develop their speaking and writing skills. She and her husband, Gene, founded the nonprofit organization Speak Up for Hope, which benefits inmates and their families.

She holds a master's degree in communication arts and a bachelor's degree in speech education. She is a former radio show cohost and has often been a guest on Focus on the Family and many other media outlets.

Carol has trained Christian speakers for over twenty-five years. She has been a featured speaker at Women of Faith, Extraordinary Women, and Women of Joy arena events. She is the author of over twenty-five books, including the best-selling *When I Lay My Isaac Down* and *Becoming a Woman of Influence* (NavPress), a 365 page-per-day devotional titled *He Walks with Me* (Christian Art Gifts), and the 2021 Christian Market Christian Living Book of the Year, *Staying Power: Building a Stronger Marriage When Life Sends Its Worst* (Revell, coauthored with Gene Kent and Cindy and David Lambert), and *Life Lessons for Moms* (Christian Art Gifts).

She and Gene are both fans of tracking down the best cup of coffee in every city they visit. Their favorite activity is watching sunsets together.

Connect with Carol

www.facebook.com/AuthorCarolKent
www.X.com/CarolKentSpeaks
www.instagram.com/CarolKentSpeaks
www.CarolKent.org
www.SpeakUpMinistries.com
www.SpeakUpConference.com
www.SpeakUpforHope.org
For information, call 586.481.7661.

About Gracie Malone

It wasn't until after her youngest son headed off to college that Gracie mailed an article she'd written to a magazine. She wondered if, just maybe, they'd be interested in publishing it. They were! (There's life after kids.) Her first article came out in *Moody Magazine*.

Since then, Gracie's work has been published several times in *Moody* and in other well-known magazines, including *Discipleship Journal*, *Decision*, *Women Alive*, *Christian Parenting Today*, *Home Life*, *Celebrate Life*, and *The Virtuous Woman*.

Courage for the Chicken-Hearted, Gracie's first book project, coauthored with four friends affectionately dubbed "Hens with Pens," quickly became a bestseller. The success of her first book encouraged its sequel the next year, *Eggstra*

Courage for the Chicken-Hearted.

Gracie's works include *Off My Rocker: Grandparenting Ain't What It Used to Be; Still Making Waves: Creating a Splash in Midlife and Beyond*; and *Unafraid: 365 Days Without Fear.*

She has contributed to several other books, including *It Took This Long to Learn This Much, Humor for a Mom's Heart, Humor for a Woman's Heart,* and the Women of Faith compilation *She Who Laughs, Lasts.*

Gracie hails from Grapevine, Texas, and she's become known as a specialist on the topic of grandparenting—hence, the book now in your hands.

She says, "May God bless you and your little ones, and bring you joy!"

Contributors

Annetta Dellinger is known as "The JOY Lady." She has coauthored three books and is now the manager of volunteers for a hospice agency. Her mission is to encourage grandparents to make memories for their family through the everyday things they say and do. Annetta is the grandmother of four and the great grandmother of four.

Jennie Afman Dimkoff is an author and international speaker for retreats, conferences, and events on college campuses. She serves on the boards of Our Daily Bread Global Ministries and Speak Up for Hope. She is also on the faculty at the annual Speak Up Conference. Her website is www.JennieDimkoff.com.

Bonnie Afman Emmorey is the conference director for the Speak Up Conference, a ministry that equips Christian speakers and writers. She's also the director of Speak Up for Hope, a prison ministry. Bonnie and her husband, Ron, have two grown sons, two awesome daughters-in-law, and six delightful grands. They reside in Wichita, Kansas.

Judy Hampton was a public speaker and Bible teacher who taught powerful principles with a touch of humor and an emphasis on the Word of God. She spoke internationally for women's conferences and authored the book *Under the Circumstances*. Judy has left her earth shackles for heaven, and she is greatly missed.

Phyllis Harmony loves the common stuff of everyday life. She believes God's Word gives meaningful definition to everyday life and that real-life experiences provide us with opportunities to live out important biblical principles. She shares memorable stories and applies God's truth to daily life in ways that are enlightening and encouraging.

Luan Zemmer Jackson, MS, RN, CS is a "people builder," and helps clients communicate effectively, resolve conflict, manage stress, and achieve balance in life. She is a nurse entrepreneur and established a full-service mental health clinic, where she continues to maintain a caseload of clients. She's an international speaker and has two children and seven grandchildren.

Ginger Kamps is a retired senior executive secretary at the Kellogg Company. She lives in Michigan with her husband, Kenny. Together they share ten grandchildren. Her current writing project is chronicling her and her husband's adventure through Alzheimer's disease.

Laura Lee Leathers is an award-winning writer and speaker. At this "age and stage" of her life, Laura's desire is "Helping You Flourish in Faith & Finish Well by His Word." But her favorite activity is hosting Nana's Weekend for her grandchildren. Find her at www.lauraleeleathers.com.

Heidi McLaughlin is an author and international speaker who lives in British Columbia, Canada, and has been widowed twice. She is the mom and stepmom of an eclectic blended family of five children and twelve grandchildren, who provide her with endless humor and stories.

Shari Minke believes with God, ALL things are possible! He has transformed her from a shy, fear-filled person to a faith-filled speaker. Shari has a passion for encouraging others into a deeper walk with Jesus Christ. She and her husband, Tom, have four children and nine grandchildren.

Linda Neff is a wife, mother, grandmother, and writer who lives north of Toronto, Ontario, Canada. She retired from more than twenty years of teaching at both elementary and secondary school levels. These experiences, plus reading and travel, have given her much material for laughing, learning, and praying.

Diana Pintar is the past president of Next Step Ministries, Inc. She has been a women's ministries director and a national speaker. Diana was also on the faculty of Speak Up

Ministries, equipping the next generation of Christian communicators. She loves discipling, coaching, and encouraging women to follow hard after God.

Bobbie Rill, MA, LPC is the clinical director of Arizona Family Counseling, Southern Region, a ministry of Christian Family Care. She has worked as a conference director, speaker, leader, and counselor through Christian ministries for most of her adult life. She resides in Tucson, Arizona.

Ginger Shaw serves as President of California Against Slavery and chair of the Southern California Safe Shelter Collaborative that locates shelter for survivors of abuse and exploitation. She is a speaker, educator, and advocate who believes the power of story reaches people of all ages and cultures.

Cynthia Spell is a Christian counselor, keynote speaker, and the author of *Deceived by Shame, Desired by God*. Her heart's desire is to teach women this truth: there is nothing you've done that is beyond God's redemption. He can turn our brokenness into a beautiful mosaic masterpiece.

Debi Stack is an active writer and career communicator based in Kansas City, Missouri. She has published hundreds of articles and several books under her own name and as a ghostwriter.

Vicki Tiede is an author, speaker, and owner of a health coaching business. As a champion of truth, hope, and health, she mentors and equips others to fulfill God's plan in their lives by stewarding their health. Vicki wrote *When Your Husband Is Addicted to Pornography: Healing Your Wounded Heart*.

Jeanne Zornes, of Washington state, has written *When I Prayed for Patience … God Let Me Have It*; *When I Got on the Highway to Heaven … I Didn't Expect Rocky Roads*; *When I Felt Like Ragweed God, Saw a Rose*; and *Spiritual Spandex for the Outstretched Soul*. Her weekly blog can be found at www.jeannezornes.blogspot.com.